TAXONOMY
OF
EDUCATIONAL OBJECTIVES

The Classification of Educational Goals

TAXONOMY

OF

EDUCATIONAL OBJECTIVES

The Classification of Educational Goals

HANDBOOK 1   COGNITIVE DOMAIN

By

A Committee of College
and University Examiners

Benjamin S. Bloom, Editor
University of Chicago

Max D. Engelhart
Duke University

Edward J. Furst
University of Arkansas

Walker H. Hill
Michigan State University

David R. Krathwohl
Syracuse University

LONGMAN GROUP LTD
LONDON

LONGMAN GROUP LIMITED
London
Associated companies, branches and representatives
throughout the world

TAXONOMY OF
EDUCATIONAL OBJECTIVES

Handbook 1: Cognitive Domain

Eighteenth Printing, May 1974

SPCK £2.25 9/76.
370.1   3/3819

ISBN: 0-582-32386-X

Library of Congress Catalog Card Number: 64-12369

Manufactured in the United States of America

To Ralph W. Tyler,
whose ideas on evaluation have been
a constant source of stimulation to
his colleagues in examining, and whose
energy and patience have never failed us.

List of participants who contributed
to the development of the taxonomy
through attending one or more of the
conferences held from 1949 to 1953

Anderson, Gordon V.
University of Texas

Bloom, Benjamin S.
University of Chicago

Churchill, Ruth
Antioch College

Cronbach, L. J.
University of Illinois

Dahnke, Harold L., Jr.
Michigan State University

Detchen, Lily
Pennsylvania College
    for Women

Dressel, Paul L.
Michigan State University

Dyer, Henry S.
Educational Testing Service

Ebel, Robert L.
University of Iowa

Engelhart, Max
Chicago Public Schools

Findley, Warren
Educational Testing Service

Furst, Edward J.
University of Michigan

Gage, N. L.
University of Illinois

Harris, Chester W.
University of Wisconsin

Hastings, J. Thomas
University of Illinois

Heil, Louis M.
Brooklyn College

Hill, Walker H.
Michigan State University

Horton, Clark W.
Dartmouth College

Krathwohl, David R.
Michigan State University

Loree, M. Ray
Louisiana State University

Mayhew, Louis B.
Michigan State University

McGuire, Christine
University of Chicago

McQuitty, John V.
University of Florida

Morris, John B.
University of Mississippi

Plumlee, Lynnette
Educational Testing Service

Pace, C. Robert
Syracuse University

Remmers, H. H.
Purdue University

Stern, George G.
Syracuse University

Sutton, Robert B.
Ohio State University

Thiede, Wilson
University of Wisconsin

Travers, Robert M.
Human Resources Research Center
San Antonio, Texas

Tyler, Ralph W.
Center for Advanced Study in the Behavioral Sciences
Stanford, California

Warrington, Willard G.
Michigan State University

*Watt, Rex
University of Southern California

---

*Deceased

CONTENTS

PART I
Introduction and Explanation

PART II
The Taxonomy and Illustrative Materials

PART I

INTRODUCTION
AND
EXPLANATION

FOREWORD

Taxonomy--"Classification, esp. of animals and plants according to their natural relationships ... "[1]

Most readers will have heard of the biological taxonomies which permit classification into such categories as phyllum, class, order, family, genus, species, variety. Biologists have found their taxonomy markedly helpful as a means of insuring accuracy of communication about their science and as a means of understanding the organization and interrelation of the various parts of the animal and plant world.   You are reading about an attempt to build a taxonomy of educational objectives.   It is intended to provide for classification of the goals of our educational system. It is expected to be of general help to all teachers, administrators, professional specialists, and research workers who deal with curricular and evaluation problems.   It is especially intended to help them discuss these problems with greater precision.   For example, some teachers believe their students should "really understand," others desire their students to "internalize knowledge," still others want their students to "grasp the core or essence" or "comprehend." Do they all mean the same thing? Specifically, what does a student do who "really understands" which he does not do when he does not understand? Through reference to the taxonomy as a set of standard classifications, teachers should be able to define such nebulous terms as those given above.   This should facilitate the exchange of information about their curricular developments and evaluation devices. Such interchanges are frequently disappointing now because all too frequently what appears to be common ground between schools disappears on closer examination of the descriptive terms being used.

But beyond this, the taxonomy should be a source of constructive help on these problems.   Teachers building a

---

[1] Webster's New Collegiate Dictionary, Springfield, Mass.: G. & C. Merriam Co., 1953, p. 871.

1

curriculum should find here a range of possible educational goals or outcomes in the cognitive area ("cognitive" is used to include activities such as remembering and recalling knowledge, thinking, problem solving, creating). Comparing the goals of their present curriculum with the range of possible outcomes may suggest additional goals they may wish to include. As a further aid, sample objectives chosen from a range of subject-matter fields (though mostly from the upper educational levels) are used to illustrate each of the taxonomy categories. These may be suggestive of the kinds of objectives that could be included in their own curriculum.

Use of the taxonomy can also help one gain a perspective on the emphasis given to certain behaviors by a particular set of educational plans. Thus, a teacher, in classifying the goals of a teaching unit, may find that they all fall within the taxonomy category of recalling or remembering knowledge. Looking at the taxonomy categories may suggest to him that, for example, he could include some goals dealing with the application of this knowledge and with the analysis of the situations in which the knowledge is used.

Curriculum builders should find the taxonomy helps them to specify objectives so that it becomes easier to plan learning experiences and prepare evaluation devices. To return to the illustration of the use of the term "understanding," a teacher might use the taxonomy to decide which of several meanings he intended. If it meant that the student was sufficiently aware of a situation or phenomenon to describe it in terms slightly different from those originally used in describing it, this would correspond to the taxonomy category of "Translation." Deeper understanding would be reflected in the next-higher level of the taxonomy, "Interpretation," where the student would be expected to summarize and explain the phenomenon in his description. And there are other levels of the taxonomy which the teacher could use to indicate still deeper "understanding." In short, teachers and curriculum makers should find this a relatively concise model for the analysis of educational outcomes in the cognitive area of remembering, thinking, and problem solving.

Once they have classified the objectives they wish to measure, teachers and testers working on evaluation problems may refer to the discussions of the problems of measuring such objectives. The Handbook includes constructive suggestions for measuring each class of objectives and offers a number of examples of the different item types which have been used by examiners.

Some research workers have found the categories of use as a framework for viewing the educational process and analyzing its workings. For instance, the AERA Committee on Criteria of Teacher Effectiveness suggests its use in analyzing the teacher's success in classroom teaching.[2] Bloom used them in analyzing the kinds of learning that take place in class discussions.[3] Equally important, the psychological relationships employed by the classification scheme are suggestive of psychological investigations which could further our understanding of the educational process and provide insight into the means by which the learner changes in a specified direction.

But any of these uses demands a clear understanding of the structure of the taxonomy, its principles of construction, and its organization. We hope this can be easily acquired by a study of the introductory chapters. In addition, it is suggested that the reader refer early and repeatedly to the condensed version of the taxonomy which has been placed at the back of the book in an appendix for easy reference. The condensed version gives an over-all view of the classification system, brief definitions of the categories, and a few examples of the objectives belonging in each category. For quick reference and a general grasp of the project, the condensed version of the taxonomy will be found to be one of the most valuable parts of the book. The brief overview of historical background plus the description of problems and of the organization of the taxonomy project found in the remainder of this Foreword should further

---

[2] Remmers, H. H., et al, "Report of the Committee on the Criteria of Teacher Effectiveness," Review of Educational Research, 22 (1952), pp. 245, 246.

[3] Bloom, B. S., "The Thought Processes of Students in Discussion," in Sydney J. French, Accent on Teaching, New York: Harper & Bros., 1954.

orient the reader. Part I of the Handbook is intended to develop some insight into the principles of development and organization of the taxonomy, to develop an understanding of the nature and significance of the cognitive domain, and to give some help on the manner in which objectives may be classified in the taxonomy.

Part II is the taxonomy proper. It consists of the taxonomy categories, sequentially arranged as listed in the condensed version and in the Table of Contents. Each one of the categories contains, in order: (1) a definition of the category; (2) illustrative objectives; (3) a discussion of problems and considerations in testing objectives in the category; and (4) examples of items testing objectives in the category. Each test example is briefly discussed to note what is required of the student and how this is achieved.

History

The idea for this classification system was formed at an informal meeting of college examiners attending the 1948 American Psychological Association Convention in Boston. At this meeting, interest was expressed in a theoretical framework which could be used to facilitate communication among examiners. This group felt that such a framework could do much to promote the exchange of test materials and ideas about testing. In addition, it could be helpful in stimulating research on examining and on the relations between examining and education. After considerable discussion, there was agreement that such a theoretical framework might best be obtained through a system of classifying the goals of the educational process, since educational objectives provide the basis for building curricula and tests and represent the starting point for much of our educational research.

This meeting became the first of a series of informal annual meetings of college examiners. Gathering at a different university each year and with some changes in membership, this group has considered the problems involved in organizing a classification of educational objectives. The group has also considered a great many other problems of examining and of educational research. This is the first product of these meetings.

The committee named on the title page was delegated the task of organizing and writing the various parts of the "cognitive" portion of the taxonomy, while the group continued in its efforts to develop the "affective" portion of the taxonomy. As yet, however, the group is still an informal one without dues, regular membership, or the usual offi- cers. Under such conditions, the committee and the editor must take responsibility for the present product, although "credit" for ideas, suggestions, and sound criticism should be distributed more widely among all those who have at- tended one or more meetings of the group.

Problems

One of the first problems raised in our discussions was whether or not educational objectives could be classi- fied. It was pointed out that we were attempting to classify phenomena which could not be observed or manipulated in the same concrete form as the phenomena of such fields as the physical and biological sciences, where taxonomies of a very high order have already been developed. Neverthe- less, it was the view of the group that educational objectives stated in behavioral form have their counterparts in the behavior of individuals. Such behavior can be observed and described, and these descriptive statements can be classified.

There was some concern expressed in the early meet- ings that the availability of the taxonomy might tend to abort the thinking and planning of teachers with regard to curric- ulum, particularly if teachers merely selected what they believed to be desirable objectives from the list provided in the taxonomy. The process of thinking about educational objectives, defining them, and relating them to teaching and testing procedures was regarded as a very important step on the part of teachers. It was suggested that the taxonomy could be most useful to teachers who have already gone through some of the steps in thinking about educational ob- jectives and curriculum.

Some fear was expressed that the taxonomy might lead to fragmentation and atomization of educational purposes such that the parts and pieces finally placed into the classification might be very different from the more complete objective with which one started. Although this was recognized as a very real danger, one solution for this problem appeared to be setting the taxonomy at a level of generality where the loss by fragmentation would not be too great. The provision of major categories as well as subcategories in the taxonomy enables the user of the taxonomy to select the level of classification which does least violence to the statement of the objective. Further, the hierarchical character of the taxonomy enables the user to more clearly understand the place of a particular objective in relation to other objectives.

Organizational principles

In discussing the principles by which a taxonomy might be developed, it was agreed that the taxonomy should be an educational - logical - psychological classification system. The terms in this order express the emphasis placed on the different principles by which the taxonomy could be developed. Thus, first importance should be given to educational considerations. Insofar as possible, the boundaries between categories should be closely related to the distinctions teachers make in planning curricula or in choosing learning situations. It is possible that teachers make distinctions which psychologists would not make in classifying or studying human behavior. However, if one of the major values of the taxonomy is in the improvement of communication among educators, then educational distinctions should be given major consideration. Second, the taxonomy should be a logical classification in that every effort should be made to define terms as precisely as possible and to use them consistently. Finally, the taxonomy should be consistent with relevant and accepted psychological principles and theories.

It was further agreed that in constructing the taxonomy every effort should be made to avoid value judgments about objectives and behaviors. Neutrality with respect to educational principles and philosophies was to be achieved by constructing a system which, insofar as it was possible, would permit the inclusion of objectives from all educational orientations. Thus, it should be possible to classify all objectives which can be stated as descriptions of student behavior.

Three domains--cognitive, affective, and psychomotor

Our original plans called for a complete taxonomy in three major parts--the cognitive, the affective, and the psychomotor domains. The cognitive domain, which is the concern of this Handbook, includes those objectives which deal with the recall or recognition of knowledge and the development of intellectual abilities and skills. This is the domain which is most central to the work of much current test development. It is the domain in which most of the work in curriculum development has taken place and where the clearest definitions of objectives are to be found phrased as descriptions of student behavior. For these reasons we started our work here, and this is the first of our work to be published.

A second part of the taxonomy is the affective domain. It includes objectives which describe changes in interest, attitudes, and values, and the development of appreciations and adequate adjustment. Much of our meeting time has been devoted to attempts at classifying objectives under this domain. It has been a difficult task which is still far from complete. Several problems make it so difficult. Objectives in this domain are not stated very precisely; and, in fact, teachers do not appear to be very clear about the learning experiences which are appropriate to these objectives. It is difficult to describe the behaviors appropriate to these objectives since the internal or covert feelings and emotions are as significant for this domain as are the overt behavioral manifestations. Then, too, our testing procedures for the affective domain are still in the most primitive stages. We hope to complete the task but are not able to predict a publication date.

A third domain is the manipulative or motor-skill area. Although we recognize the existence of this domain, we find so little done about it in secondary schools or colleges, that we do not believe the development of a classification of these objectives would be very useful at present. We would appreciate comments on this point from teachers and other educational workers who are especially interested in this domain of educational objectives.

Development of the cognitive domain

We were naturally hesitant about publishing the cognitive-domain handbook without securing as widespread comment and criticism as possible. Members of the group have discussed the taxonomy with their colleagues in their own institutions, with graduate students in curriculum and testing, and with other groups of teachers and educational specialists. The criticisms and suggestions of these groups have, whenever possible, been taken into consideration in the present volume. A somewhat more formal presentation was made in a symposium at the American Psychological Association meetings in Chicago in 1951.[4]

In spite of these means of communication, we still felt the need for the comments, suggestions, and criticisms of a larger and more representative group of educators, teachers, and educational research workers. With this in mind, we were very pleased when Longmans, Green and Company agreed to print a preliminary edition of 1000 copies before printing the final version of the Handbook. The preliminary edition was sent to a large group of college and secondary school teachers, administrators, curriculum directors, and educational research specialists. This group was asked to read the preliminary edition carefully and to offer criticisms and suggestions, as well as additional illustrations of objectives and test materials. They responded very generously and the present version of the Handbook has taken many of their ideas into consideration. We are truly grateful for the time and thought given to this work.

---

[4] Symposium: The Development of a Taxonomy of Educational Objectives, H. H. Remmers, Chairman. Participants: B. S. Bloom, Intellectual domain; D. R. Krathwohl, Affective domain. Discussants: O. K. Buros, O. H. Mowrer, and J. M. Stalnaker. Fifty-ninth Annual Meeting of the American Psychological Association, August 31-September 5, Chicago, Illinois.

Thus, this Handbook is truly a group product. It is the direct outgrowth of the thinking of over thirty persons who attended the taxonomy conferences. It is based on the work of countless test constructors, curriculum workers, and teachers. Several hundred readers of the preliminary edition have contributed criticisms, suggestions, and illustrative materials. The committee which took responsibility for the actual writing hope that this Handbook justifies the enormous amount of time and effort devoted to it by the many persons involved. We regard the work as well worth the effort if the taxonomy is found of value as a means of communicating within the field of education. We submit it in the hope that it will help to stimulate thought and research on educational problems.

Since this is a handbook in which a classification scheme is described and illustrated, the reader is cautioned against attempting to read it as though it were a narrative or an exposition of a point of view which could easily be read from cover to cover. The reader may find it profitable to read the introduction and the condensed version of the taxonomy in the Appendix in order to get a quick overview of the entire book. The chapter on educational objectives and curriculum development followed by the chapter on the classification of educational objectives and test exercises will enable him to secure a more thorough understanding of the taxonomy and its possible uses. The remaining sections of the volume--the taxonomy with illustrative objectives and test items--should be read as the reader finds these sections relevant to specific teaching, curriculum, testing and research problems.

CHAPTER 1

THE NATURE AND DEVELOPMENT
OF THE TAXONOMY

The taxonomy as a classification device

The major purpose in constructing a taxonomy of educational objectives is to facilitate communication. In our original consideration of the project we conceived of it as a method of improving the exchange of ideas and materials among test workers, as well as other persons concerned with educational research and curriculum development. For instance, the use of the taxonomy as an aid in developing a precise definition and classification of such vaguely defined terms as "thinking" and "problem solving" would enable a group of schools to discern the similarities and differences among the goals of their different instructional programs. They could compare and exchange tests and other evaluative devices intended to determine the effectiveness of these programs. They could, therefore, begin to understand more completely the relation between the learning experiences provided by these various programs and the changes which take place in their students.

Set at this level, the task of producing a taxonomy, that is, a classification of educational outcomes, is quite analogous to the development of a plan for classifying books in a library. Or, put more abstractly, it is like establishing symbols for designating classes of objects where the members of a class have something in common. In a library these symbols might be the words "fiction" and "nonfiction" and would apply to classes of books having something in common. If the problem is essentially one of finding new symbols for the classes, any set of symbols, numbers, nonsense syllables, or words could be used. Thus, we could have used the symbols "F" and "NF" for fiction and nonfiction. Further, since the symbols selected are not intended to convey that one class is of a higher order than another or that there is any particular relationship between the classes, they can be selected in very arbitrary fashion.

The labels "fiction" and "nonfiction" do not imply that the one class of book is better, more abstract, or more complex than the other kind.

Of course, such a classification procedure cannot be a private fantasy since it is of value only if used by the workers who wish to communicate with each other. Thus, the classifications "fiction" and "nonfiction" are of value only if librarians use them. Acceptance of such classifications by potential users is likely to be facilitated if the class names are terms which are reasonably familiar to them and if these terms are given precise and usable definitions. Thus, one might expect more ready acceptance of a library classification scheme if he took such a term as "fiction," which is already in use, and defined it so that any competent librarian would easily be able to determine which books fit the classification.

In summary then, the major task in setting up any kind of taxonomy is that of selecting appropriate symbols, giving them precise and usable definitions, and securing the consensus of the group which is to use them. Similarly, developing a classification of educational objectives requires the selection of an appropriate list of symbols to represent all the major types of educational outcomes. Next, there is the task of defining these symbols with sufficient precision to permit and facilitate communication about these phenomena among teachers, administrators, curriculum workers, testers, educational research workers, and others who are likely to use the taxonomy. Finally, there is the task of trying the classification and securing the consensus of the educational workers who wish to use the taxonomy.

What is to be classified

Before one can build a classification scheme, it must be clear what it is that is to be classified. This is not much of a problem when one is classifying books. But descriptions of curricula are set up on such different bases as descriptions of teacher behavior, descriptions of instructional methods, and descriptions of intended pupil behaviors. As achievement testers and educational research workers, the major phenomena with which we are concerned are the changes produced in individuals as a result of educational experiences. Such changes may be represented by the global statements of the educational objectives of an educational unit, or they may be represented by the actual description of the student behaviors which are regarded as appropriate or relevant to the objectives. Objectives may also be inferred from the tasks, problems, and observations used to test or evaluate the presence of these behaviors.

We are of the opinion that although the objectives and test materials and techniques may be specified in an almost unlimited number of ways, the student behaviors involved in these objectives can be represented by a relatively small number of classes. Therefore, this taxonomy is designed to be a classification of the student behaviors which represent the intended outcomes of the educational process. It is assumed that essentially the same classes of behavior may be observed in the usual range of subject-matter content, at different levels of education (elementary, high-school, college), and in different schools. Thus, a single set of classifications should be applicable in all these instances.

It should be noted that we are not attempting to classify the instructional methods used by teachers, the ways in which teachers relate themselves to students, or the different kinds of instructional materials they use. We are not attempting to classify the particular subject matter or content. What we are classifying is the intended behavior of students--the ways in which individuals are to act, think, or feel as the result of participating in some unit of instruction. (Only such of these intended behaviors as are related to mental acts or thinking are included in the part of the taxonomy developed in this Handbook.)

It is recognized that the actual behaviors of the students after they have completed the unit of instruction may differ in degree as well as in kind from the intended behaviors specified by the objectives. That is, the effects of instruction may be such that the students do not learn a given skill to the desired level of perfection; or, for that matter, they may not develop the intended skill to any degree.

This is a matter of grading or evaluating the goodness of the performance. The emphasis in the Handbook is on obtaining evidence on the extent to which desired and intended behaviors have been learned by the student. It is outside the scope of the task we set ourselves to properly treat the matter of determining the appropriate value to be placed on the different degrees of achievement of the objectives of instruction.

It should also be noted that the intended behaviors specified by educational objectives do not include many of the behaviors which psychologists are interested in classifying and studying. One reason is that the intended behaviors represent the social goals imposed upon youngsters by their society or culture. Thus, the intended or desired behaviors included in educational objectives usually do not include undesirable or abnormal behaviors which are socially disapproved. Similarly, certain natural or unsocialized behaviors which might be of interest to psychologists may fall outside the categories of the taxonomy.

Our present studies of the affective area have indicated that the selective nature of intended behaviors will be even more apparent there than in the cognitive domain. The fact that we include objectives which specify social and emotional adjustment as a part of the affective domain points up this fact.

Guiding principles

Since the determination of classes and their titles is in some ways arbitrary, there could be an almost infinite number of ways of dividing and naming the domains of educational outcomes. To guide us in our selection of a single classification system and to make the product more readily understood and used, we established certain guiding principles. First, since the taxonomy is to be used in regard to existing educational units and programs, we are of the opinion that the major distinctions between classes should reflect, in large part, the distinctions teachers make among student behaviors. These distinctions are revealed in the ways teachers state educational objectives. They are also found in their curricular plans, their instructional material, and their instructional methods. To the extent it was possible, the subdivisions of the taxonomy are intended to recognize these distinctions.

A second principle is that the taxonomy should be logically developed and internally consistent. Thus, each term should be defined and used in a consistent way throughout the taxonomy. In addition, each category should permit logical subdivisions which can be clearly defined and further subdivided to the extent that appears necessary and useful.

A third principle is that the taxonomy should be consistent with our present understanding of psychological phenomena. Those distinctions which are psychologically untenable, even though regularly made by teachers, would be avoided. Further, distinctions which seem psychologically important, even though not frequently made in educational objectives, would be favorably considered for inclusion. Perhaps it should be reiterated that, since the taxonomy deals only with educationally intended behavior, it falls considerably short of being a classification scheme for all psychological phenomena.

A fourth principle is that the classification should be a purely descriptive scheme in which every type of educational goal can be represented in a relatively neutral fashion. Thus, the Dewey decimal classification system for libraries describes all the classes of books. It does not indicate the value or quality of one class as compared with another, nor does it specify the number and kind of books any particular library should possess. Similarly, to avoid partiality to one view of education as opposed to another, we have attempted to make the taxonomy neutral by avoiding terms which implicitly convey value judgments and by making the taxonomy as inclusive as possible. This means that the kinds of behavioral changes emphasized by any institution, educational unit, or educational philosophy can be represented in the classification. Another way of saying this is that any objective which describes an intended behavior should be classifiable in this system. On the other hand, the taxonomy will probably include a greater variety of behaviors than those emphasized by any one school, course, or educational philosophy. Thus, one course might have objectives classifiable in four of the categories, another in only three of the categories, and so on.

In one sense, however, the taxonomy is not completely neutral. This stems from the already-noted fact that it is a classification of intended behaviors. It cannot be used to classify educational plans which are made in such a way that either the student behaviors cannot be specified or only a single (unanalyzed) term or phrase such as "understanding," or "desirable citizen," is used to describe the outcomes. Only those educational programs which can be specified in terms of intended student behaviors can be classified.

Developing the taxonomy

Keeping in mind the aforementioned principles, we began work by gathering a large list of educational objectives from our own institutions and the literature. We determined which part of the objective stated the behavior intended and which stated the content or object of the behavior. We then attempted to find divisions or groups into which the behaviors could be placed. We initially limited ourselves to those objectives commonly referred to as knowledge, intellectual abilities, and intellectual skills. (This area, which we named the cognitive domain, may also be described as including the behaviors: remembering; reasoning; problem solving; concept formation; and, to a limited extent, creative thinking.) We proceeded to divide the cognitive objectives into subdivisions from the simplest behavior to the most complex. We then attempted to find ways of defining these subdivisions in such a way that all of us working with the material could communicate with each other about the specific objectives as well as the testing procedures to be included.

We have not succeeded in finding a method of classification which would permit complete and sharp distinctions among behaviors. (This is discussed in more detail in Chapter 3, which considers the problem of classifying objectives and test exercises.) There are two basic views. First, we were again made aware of what any teacher knows—two boys may appear to be doing the same thing;

but if we analyze the situation, we find they are not. For example, two students solve an algebra problem. One student may be solving it from memory, having had the identical problem in class previously. The other student has never met the problem before and must reason out the solution by applying general principles. We can only distinguish between their behaviors as we analyze the relation between the problem and each student's background of experience. This then introduces a new aspect to the classification problem, namely, the experiential backgrounds of the students to whom the objective is to apply. As is indicated in Chapter 3, this may be a very important factor in using the taxonomy to classify test exercises.

A second difficulty in classification results from the fact that the more complex behaviors include the simpler behaviors. If we view statements of educational objectives as intended behaviors which the student shall display at the end of some period of education, we can then view the process as one of change. As teachers we intend the learning experiences to change the student's behavior from a simpler type to another more complex one which in some ways at least will include the first type.

One may take the Gestalt point of view that the complex behavior is more than the sum of the simpler behaviors, or one may view the complex behavior as being completely analyzable into simpler components. But either way, so long as the simpler behaviors may be viewed as components of the more complex behaviors, we can view the educational process as one of building on the simpler behavior. Thus, a particular behavior which is classified in one way at a given time may develop and become integrated with other behaviors to form a more complex behavior which is classified in a different way. In order to find a single place for each type of behavior, the taxonomy must be organized from simple to complex classes of behavior. Furthermore, for consistency in classification, a rule of procedure may be adopted such that a particular behavior is placed in the most complex class which is appropriate and relevant.

But, having specified that the classes shall be arranged from simple to complex, we have exceeded the simple classification scheme which called primarily for a series of categories without order or rank. The next section addresses itself to this problem.

The problem of a hierarchy—classification versus taxonomy

We have so far used the terms "classification" and "taxonomy" more or less interchangeably. It is necessary, however, that we examine the relationship between these terms because, strictly speaking, they are not interchangeable. Taxonomies, particularly Aristotelian taxonomies, have certain structural rules which exceed in complexity the rules of a classification system. While a classification scheme may have many arbitrary elements, a taxonomy scheme may not. A taxonomy must be so constructed that the order of the terms must correspond to some "real" order among the phenomena represented by the terms. A classification scheme may be validated by reference to the criteria of communicability, usefulness, and suggestiveness; while a taxonomy must be validated by demonstrating its consistency with the theoretical views in research findings of the field it attempts to order.

As educators and specialists in research, we are interested in a long-term inquiry into the nature of the phenomena with which we deal, and no simple set of terms and definitions by itself really is a satisfactory tool in making this inquiry. We need a method of ordering phenomena such that the method of ordering reveals significant relationships among the phenomena. This is the basic problem of a taxonomy—to order phenomena in ways which will reveal some of their essential properties as well as the interrelationships among them. Members of the taxonomy group spent considerable time in attempting to find a psychological theory which would provide a sound basis for ordering the categories of the taxonomy. We reviewed theories of personality and learning but were unable to find a single view which, in our opinion, accounted for the varieties of behaviors represented in the educational objectives we attempted to classify. We were reluctantly forced to agree with Hilgard[1] that each theory of learning accounts for some phenomena very well but is less adequate in accounting for others. What is needed is a larger synthetic theory of learning than at present seems to be available. We are of the opinion that our method of ordering educational outcomes will make it possible to define

[1] Hilgard, E. R., Theories of Learning (Century Psychology Series), New York: Appleton—Century—Crofts, 1948.

the range of phenomena for which such a theory must account. The taxonomy also uses an order consistent with research findings and it should provide some clues as to the nature of the theory which may be developed. This is an extremely complex problem; and although it has probably not been solved completely satisfactorily, it is the opinion of the writers that we have made some progress toward a solution.

As the taxonomy is now organized, it contains six major classes:

1.00 Knowledge
2.00 Comprehension
3.00 Application
4.00 Analysis
5.00 Synthesis
6.00 Evaluation

Although it is possible to conceive of these major classes in several different arrangements, the present one appears to us to represent something of the hierarchical order of the different classes of objectives. As we have defined them, the objectives in one class are likely to make use of and be built on the behaviors found in the preceding classes in this list. The reader is referred to the condensed version of the taxonomy in the Appendix for a brief definition of each class and its subclasses. Fuller treatment of the taxonomy will be found in Part II of this volume.

Our attempt to arrange educational behaviors from simple to complex was based on the idea that a particular simple behavior may become integrated with other equally simple behaviors to form a more complex behavior. Thus our classifications may be said to be in the form where behaviors of type A form one class, behaviors of type AB form another class, while behaviors of type ABC form still another class. If this is the real order from simple to complex, it should be related to an order of difficulty such that problems requiring behavior A alone should be answered correctly more frequently than problems requiring AB. We have studied a large number of problems occurring in our comprehensive examinations and have found some evidence to support this hypothesis. Thus, problems requiring knowledge of specific facts are generally answered correctly more frequently than problems requiring a knowledge of the universals and abstractions in a field. Problems requiring knowledge of principles and concepts are correctly answered more frequently than problems requiring both knowledge of the principle and some ability to apply it in new situations. Problems requiring analysis and synthesis are more difficult than problems requiring comprehension. Scatter plots of the performances of individuals on one test composed of items at a simple level in the taxonomy against their performances on another test composed of items at a more complex level in the taxonomy show that it is more common to find that individuals have low scores on complex problems and high scores on the less complex problems than the reverse. Our evidence on this is not entirely satisfactory, but there is an unmistakable trend pointing toward a hierarchy of classes of behavior which is in accordance with our present tentative classification of these behaviors.

While we have been primarily concerned with the cognitive domain, we have done some thinking about the classification versus taxonomy problem as it applies to all the domains. The arrangement of behaviors from simple to complex and the differentiation of behaviors into three domains—the cognitive, the psychomotor, and the affective—were made primarily from an educational viewpoint. That is, these are the distinctions which teachers make in the development of curriculum and teaching procedures. We as educational testers also make similar distinctions. As we examine the classification system so far developed, however, we note an additional dimension not usually considered in educational and teaching procedures. One of the major threads running through all the taxonomy appears to be a scale of consciousness or awareness. Thus, the behaviors in the cognitive domain are largely characterized by a rather high degree of consciousness on the part of the individual exhibiting the behavior, while the behaviors in the affective domain are much more frequently exhibited with a low level of awareness on the part of the individual. Further, in the cognitive domain especially, it appears that as the behaviors become more complex, the individual is more aware of their existence. We are of the opinion that this applies to the other domains as well. Clearly there is no precise scale of consciousness which may be used to test these speculations. However, some of our research on the thought processes involved in problem solving[2] indicates that students are able to give more complete reports of their attack on a problem as the problem becomes more complex, that is, as the problem is classified in the more complex classes of intellectual abilities and skills.

If the level of consciousness can be demonstrated to be an important dimension in the classification of behavior, it would pose a great range of problems and point to a whole new set of relationships which would be of interest to researchers in the field of educational psychology. One might hope that it would provide a basis for explaining why behaviors which are initially displayed with a high level of consciousness become, after some time and repetition, automatic or are accompanied by a low level of consciousness. Perhaps this would provide a partial basis for explaining why some learning, especially of the affective behaviors, is so difficult. Perhaps it will also help to explain the extraordinary retention of some learning — especially of the psychomotor skills.

Is the taxonomy a useful tool?

We have subjected this classification scheme to a series of checks, primarily of communicability and comprehensiveness. A major check of communicability was to determine whether a number of workers could agree in their classification of specific educational objectives and test materials. Members of the taxonomy group discussed the classification of particular objectives in certain categories, and many ambiguities and inconsistencies were pointed out which we have attempted to remedy. Perhaps the most complete test of the classifications and their definitions has been the attempt of members of the group to classify a large number of test items. One of the major problems in the classification of test items which this study revealed is that it is necessary in all cases to know or assume the nature of the

[2] Bloom, B. S., and Broder, Lois, Problem-solving processes of college students (A Supplementary Educational Monograph), Chicago: University of Chicago Press, Summer, 1950.

examinees' prior educational experiences. Thus, a test problem could require a very complex type of problem-solving behavior if it is a new situation, while it may require little more than a simple kind of recall if the individual has had previous learning experiences in which this very problem was analyzed and discussed. This suggests that, in general, test material can be satisfactorily classified by means of the taxonomy only when the context in which the test problems were used is known or assumed.

Comprehensiveness, of course, is never finally determined. We have repeatedly taken lists of objectives found in courses of study and other educational literature and have attempted to classify them. As yet, in the cognitive domain we have encountered few statements of student behaviors which could not be placed within the classification scheme. However, although we have little difficulty in determining the major class within which a behavior falls, we still are not satisfied that there are enough clearly defined subclassifications to provide adequately for the great variety of objectives we have attempted to classify.

In addition to comprehensiveness and communicability, the taxonomy should satisfy two other criteria if it is to be regarded as a useful and effective tool. First, it should stimulate thought about educational problems. If the taxonomy is to prove a useful tool for educational research workers, it must aid them in formulating hypotheses about the learning process and changes in students. If it is to be useful for teachers and testers, it should provide a basis for suggestions as to methods for developing curricula, instructional techniques, and testing techniques. As a highly organized and presumably comprehensive plan for classifying educational behaviors, it should form the basis for easily determining the availability of relevant evaluation instruments, techniques, and methods so that each worker can determine their appropriateness for his own work. Properly used, a taxonomy should provide a very suggestive source of ideas and materials for each worker and should result in many economies in effort.

The early drafts of the taxonomy have already been extensively used. Some of the examiners have found it useful as an aid in helping the faculty formulate objectives more precisely and in seeing a possible range of educational objectives. The major categories of the taxonomy have been used in several institutions as a basis for classifying test material. The parallelism of objectives in different subject-matter fields is highlighted by this procedure, thus suggesting points of possible integration. Further, the transferability of testing techniques from one subject field to another becomes clear. In at least one institution, diagnostic reports of test results to students are made in relation to the taxonomy. In this same institution, reports to the faculty on the relation of the test results to the objectives and learning experiences are analyzed in terms of the taxonomy.

Stimulation of thought on educational problems may also occur through the use of the taxonomy in organizing some of the literature on educational research. Used in this way, it gives a relatively fresh view to some of this research and reveals many problems which have been largely ignored by educational psychologists, curriculum workers, and testers. Some of the studies on the relationship between measures of scholastic aptitude or intelligence and the evidence on the development of particular classes of behaviors have been brought together. [3] This has revealed rather strikingly the relatively low relationship between tests of some of the more complex cognitive abilities and skills and measures of intelligence. Thus, the view that measures of the higher mental processes are synonymous with measures of scholastic aptitude does not seem to be well-founded. This view has frequently been used to support the contention that, since intelligence is presumed to be constant, little can be done to develop some of the higher mental processes through educative experiences.

---

[3] Furst, Edward J., "Relationship between tests of intelligence and tests of critical thinking and knowledge," Journal of Educational Research, Vol. 43, No. 8, April 1950, pp. 614-25.

Available evidence has also been assembled on the interrelations among educational objectives. [4,5] These data give considerable support to the generalization that the relationships among measures of different objectives are determined by the nature of the learning experiences which the students have had. Thus, it seems possible under one curriculum to integrate various behaviors in such a way that very high correlations are obtained among the measures of the different objectives while under another curricular plan the correlations among the measures of the different objectives do not depart very much from chance. This has been a long-neglected area in curricular planning and educational research.

We have also attempted to organize some of the literature on the growth, retention, and transfer of the different types of educational outcomes or behaviors. Here we find very little relevant research. [6] For the most part, research on problems in retention, growth, and transfer has not been very specific with respect to the particular behavior involved. Thus, we are usually not able to determine from this research whether one kind of behavior is retained for a longer period of time than another or which kinds of educative experiences are most efficient in producing a particular kind of behavior. Many claims have been made for different educational procedures, particularly in relation to permanence of learning; but seldom have these been buttressed by research findings.

Altogether, the taxonomy is suggestive in pointing to a large number of problems in the field of education and testing. If the taxonomy could do nothing more than this, it would be useful. Although there are dangers in devising

[4] Furst, Edward J., "Effect of the organization of learning experiences upon the organization of learning outcomes," Journal of Experimental Education, XVIII (March 1954), pp. 215-28.

[5] Dressel, Paul L., and Mayhew, Lewis B., General Education: Explorations in Evaluation, Washington, D. C.: American Council on Education, 1954, pp. 249-53.

[6] Several of the more relevant references are listed in the footnotes on page 42.

a classification scheme which might tend to rigidify our thinking about education, the relatively chaotic nature of our field at present and the great emphasis on persuasive skills rather than on research findings for claims in the field of education justify some procedure such as this for ordering the phenomena with which we deal.

A final criterion is that the taxonomy must be accepted and used by the workers in the field if it is to be regarded as a useful and effective tool. Whether or not it meets this criterion can be determined only after a sufficient amount of time has elapsed. We have attempted to secure the participation of a large number of achievement testers and evaluation specialists in the actual development and criticism of the classification scheme. The bulk of the comments from administrators, teachers, curriculum specialists, and educational research workers on the preliminary edition of the taxonomy indicate that there is a real need for this kind of device. We do not regard it as perfect or as completed. We expect to continue to work on the development of the other domains and to revise this Handbook as experience dictates the need for improvement. We solicit your help in its further development by asking that you send us the suggestions which occur to you as you attempt to understand it and as you develop a body of experience through its use.

CHAPTER 2

EDUCATIONAL OBJECTIVES AND

CURRICULUM DEVELOPMENT

We have had some question about the relevance of this section in a handbook devoted to the details of a classification system. We have finally included it because we believe the classification and evaluation of educational objectives must be considered as a part of the total process of curriculum development. Some of these considerations help to clarify the distinctions made in the taxonomy. It is hoped that many teachers will find this chapter useful as a summary of some of the arguments for inclusion of a greater range of educational objectives than is typical at the secondary school or college level.

Problems of developing curriculum and instruction are usually considered in relation to four major types of questions.[1]

1. What educational purposes or objectives should the school or course seek to attain?
2. What learning experiences can be provided that are likely to bring about the attainment of these purposes?
3. How can these learning experiences be effectively organized to help provide continuity and sequence for the learner and to help him in integrating what might otherwise appear as isolated learning experiences?
4. How can the effectiveness of learning experiences be evaluated by the use of tests and other systematic evidence-gathering procedures?

---

[1] The content of this section has been largely drawn from Ralph W. Tyler, "Achievement Testing and Curriculum Construction," Trends in Student Personnel Work, E. G. Williamson, Ed., Minneapolis, Minn.: University of Minnesota Press, 1949, pp. 391-407.

We are here concerned primarily with the first of these questions: the formulation and classification of educational objectives.

By educational objectives, we mean explicit formulations of the ways in which students are expected to be changed by the educative process. That is, the ways in which they will change in their thinking, their feelings, and their actions. There are many possible changes that can take place in students as a result of learning experiences, but since the time and resources of the school are limited, only a few of the possibilities can be realized. It is important that the major objectives of the school or unit of instruction be clearly identified if time and effort are not to be wasted on less important things and if the work of the school is to be guided by some plan.

The formulation of educational objectives is a matter of conscious choice on the part of the teaching staff, based on previous experience and aided by consideration of several kinds of data. The final selection and ordering of the objectives become a matter of making use of the learning theory and philosophy of education which the faculty accepts.

One type of source commonly used in thinking about objectives is the information available about the students. What is their present level of development? What are their needs? What are their interests? Another source for objectives is available from investigations of the conditions and problems of contemporary life which make demands on young people and adults and which provide opportunities for them. What are the activities that individuals are expected to perform? What are the problems they are likely to encounter? What are the opportunities they are likely to have for service and self-realization?

Another source of suggestions for objectives comes from the nature of the subject matter and the deliberations of subject-matter specialists on the contributions their subject is able to make to the education of the individual. What is the conception of the subject field? What are the types of learning which can arise from a study of that subject matter? What are the contributions that the subject can make in relation to other subjects?

It is likely that a consideration of these three sources will result in a suggested list of objectives which require more time and effort than the school has at its disposal. The problem of selecting among possible objectives as well as the determination of relative emphasis to be given to various objectives requires the use of some guiding conceptions. The philosophy of education of the school serves as one guide, since the objectives to be finally included should be related to the school's view of the "good life for the individual in the good society." What are the important values? What is the proper relation between man and society? What are the proper relations between man and man?

Finally, educational objectives must be related to a psychology of learning. The faculty must distinguish goals that are feasible from goals that are unlikely to be attained in the time available, under the conditions which are possible, and with the group of students to be involved. The use of a psychology of learning enables the faculty to determine the appropriate placement of objectives in the learning sequence, helps them discover the learning conditions under which it is possible to attain an objective, and provides a way of determining the appropriate interrelationships among the objectives.

It should be clear from the foregoing that objectives are not only the goals toward which the curriculum is shaped and toward which instruction is guided, but they are also the goals that provide the detailed specification for the construction and use of evaluative techniques. Several of the sources which may be of value to the reader are listed in the footnotes. [2,3,4,5,6]

---

[2] Dressel, Paul L., "Evaluation Procedures for General Education Objectives," Educational Record, April 1950, pp. 97-122.

[3] Lindquist, E. F., (Editor), Educational Measurement, Washington, D. C.: American Council on Education, 1951, chap. 5.

A test of the achievement of students is a test of the extent to which the students have attained these educational objectives. An achievement test is an adequate and valid test if it provides evidence of the extent to which students are attaining each of the major objectives of the unit of instruction.

The cognitive objectives derived from a process like that described in the foregoing paragraphs may, for discussion purposes, be divided into two parts. One would be the simple behavior of remembering or recalling knowledge and the other, the more complex behaviors of the abilities and skills. The following section discusses these two divisions in turn, considering their nature, their appearance in the taxonomy, and their place in the curriculum.

Knowledge as a taxonomy category

Probably the most common educational objective in American education is the acquisition of knowledge or information. That is, it is desired that as the result of completing an educational unit, the student will be changed with respect to the amount and kind of knowledge he possesses. Frequently knowledge is the primary, sometimes almost the sole kind of, educational objective in a curriculum. In almost every course it is an important or basic one. By knowledge, we mean that the student can give evidence that he remembers, either by recalling or by recognizing, some idea or phenomenon with which he has had experience in the educational process. For our taxonomy purposes, we are defining knowledge as little more than the remembering

---

[4] Thomas, R. Murray, Judging Student Progress, New York: Longmans, Green & Co., 1954, chap. 1.

[5] Remmers, H. H., and Gage, N. L., Educational Measurement and Evaluation, Revised Edition, New York: Harper & Bros., 1955, chap. 1.

[6] Tyler, Ralph W., and Smith, Eugene, Appraising and Recording Student Progress, Vol. III, New York: Harper & Bros., 1942, chap. 1.

of the idea or phenomenon in a form very close to that in which it was originally encountered.

This type of objective emphasizes most the psychological processes of remembering. Knowledge may also involve the more complex processes of relating and judging, since it is almost impossible to present an individual with a knowledge problem which includes exactly the same stimuli, signals, or cues as were present in the original learning situation. Thus, any test situation involving knowledge requires some organization and reorganization of the problem to furnish the appropriate signals and cues linking it to the knowledge the individual possesses. It may be helpful in this case to think of knowledge as something filed or stored in the mind. The task for the individual in each knowledge test situation is to find the appropriate signals and cues in the problem which will most effectively bring out whatever knowledge is filed or stored. For instance, almost everyone has had the experience of being unable to answer a question involving recall when the question is stated in one form, and then having little difficulty in remembering the necessary information when the question is restated in another form. This is well illustrated by John Dewey's story in which he asked a class, "What would you find if you dug a hole in the earth?" Getting no response, he repeated the question; again he obtained nothing but silence. The teacher chided Dr. Dewey, "You're asking the wrong question." Turning to the class, she asked, "What is the state of the center of the earth?" The class replied in unison, "Igneous fusion."

John Dewey's story also illustrates the rote recall nature of some knowledge learning. The emphasis on knowledge as involving little more than remembering or recall distinguishes it from those conceptions of knowledge which involve "understanding," "insight," or which are phrased as "really know," or "true knowledge." In these latter conceptions it is implicitly assumed that knowledge is of little value if it cannot be utilized in new situations or in a form very different from that in which it was originally encountered. The denotations of these latter concepts would usually be close to what have been defined as "abilities and skills" in the taxonomy.

Whether or not one accepts this latter position, it is sufficient to note that knowledge by itself is one of the most common educational objectives. The most cursory read - ing of the standardized tests available or of teacher-made tests would indicate that tremendous emphasis is given in our schools to this kind of remembering or recall. A com- prehensive taxonomy of educational objectives must, in our opinion, include all the educational objectives repre- sented in American education without making judgments about their value, meaningfulness, or appropriateness. Knowledge, therefore, is one of our taxonomy categories.

The knowledge category in particular and, as noted earlier, the classifications of the taxonomy in general range from the simple to the more complex behaviors and from the concrete or tangible to the abstract or intangible. By simple we mean elemental, isolable bits of phenomena or information, e.g., "the capital of Illinois is Springfield," or "Arkansas contains much bauxite." Thus, our base sub- classification is titled "knowledge of specifics." At the upper end of the knowledge category the subclassifications refer to more complex phenomena. Thus, remembering a theory is a more complex task than remembering a specific such as the capital of a state. Knowledge of the theory of evolution, for instance, would be very complex. Accord- ingly, the subclassification at the complex end of the knowl- edge category is titled the "knowledge of theories and structures."

The knowledge categories may also be viewed as run- ning from concrete to abstract. Thus, in general, knowl- edge of specifics will refer to concrete, tangible phenom- ena: "Insects have six legs;" "Most glass is brittle." But the more complex categories, as, for example, the name "knowledge of theories and structures" implies, tend to deal with abstract phenomena.

It might sometimes be useful for taxonomy purposes to distinguish knowledge with regard to the different speci- alties, fields of knowledge, or subdivisions of work in our schools. Thus, it would be possible to distinguish knowledge about the social sciences from knowledge about the physical sciences, and knowledge of physics from knowledge of chemistry, etc. Likewise, knowledge about man could be distinguished from knowledge about physical objects, etc. The taxonomy as developed here should be applicable to any of the subdivisions of knowledge or educational units in which school curricula are divided, but no attempt will be made to make all the possible applications or subdivisions in this Handbook. The reader may wish to develop such further classifications as are necessary for his work, using the taxonomy as a basis.

What is knowable

One of the major problems with regard to knowledge is determining what is knowable, for there are different ways in which something can be said to be known. Adding to this problem is the fact that different criteria of accuracy and authenticity are applied to knowledge in different areas, at least the knowledge to be learned in school. To a large extent knowledge, as taught in American schools, depends upon some external authority; some expert or group of experts is the arbiter of knowledge. Some information is the result of little more than convention and consensus. That is, a group of workers or experts in the field has come to some agreement on the ways in which particular terms will be defined, on the particular referents for selected symbols, or the most effective or practical ways in which to organize a field or attack problems in it. For instance, lexicographers appear to make many arbitrary decisions in preparing a dictionary. The symbol system for punctuation is solely a matter of convention. Memorizing the conjugation of verbs and the declension of nouns is accepted as the proper approach to learning some foreign languages. Other information is known as the result of logical tests of consistency either by definition or by some logic of relationship. Certain kinds of geometry, mathematical propositions, and mathematical models are examples. Finally, some knowledge or information is known as the result of some historical, experiential, or pragmatic test. Thus, historical information is known as the result of a number of observations which are in agreement or which satisfy particular historical tests of their authenticity. Scientific information is known as a result of some observation, experiment, or test which meets the canons of scientific methodology.

It should also be noted that the validity, accuracy, and meaningfulness of information are relative in many ways and always are related to a particular period of time. Thus, what is known in 1955 was not known in the same way in a previous era and will presumably undergo some changes in the future. Compare the way we pictured the atom twenty years ago with today's view of it.

There is also a geographical and cultural aspect to knowledge in the sense that what is known to one group is not necessarily known to another group, class, or culture. It must be clear from all this, that knowledge is always partial and relative rather than inclusive and fixed.

Justification for the development of knowledge

Knowledge or information may be justified as an important objective or outcome of learning in many ways. Perhaps the most common justification is that with increase in knowledge or information there is a development of one's acquaintance with reality. Such reality may represent what is known by convention or definition, what are known as the findings or outcome of inquiry in the various fields, what are known as the more fruitful ways of attacking problems in the field, or what are known as the more useful ways of organizing a field. It is assumed that as the number of things known by an individual increases, his acquaintance with the world in which he lives increases. But, as has been pointed out before, we recognize the point of view that truth and knowledge are only relative and that there are no hard and fast truths which exist for all time and all places. Nonetheless, most educators hold it desirable that the learner increase his knowledge of what is currently known or accepted by the experts or specialists in a field, whether or not such knowledge, in a philosophical sense, corresponds to "reality."

The selection of knowledge as an educational objective usually assumes some stability in the world, in the culture, or in the subject field. If the knowledge learned at one time is not regarded as very useful or accurate at another time, there would be little point in the student learning it. It is likely that the stability of knowledge varies considerably with the field or problem under consideration. Some fields or topics are undergoing such rapid transition that what is known at one time is not accepted or is altered shortly thereafter. Under such conditions the acquisition of knowledge could not be justified for its own sake but would have to be justified in relation to the other educational objectives, a position which is discussed next.

Another justification for the teaching of knowledge is that it is quite frequently regarded as basic to all the other ends or purposes of education. Problem solving or thinking cannot be carried on in a vacuum, but must be based upon knowledge of some of the "realities." The intellectual abilities represented in the taxonomy assume knowledge as a prerequisite. Knowledge becomes either the material with which the problem solving deals or it becomes the test of the adequacy and accuracy of the problem solving. Thus in fields undergoing rapid transition, knowledge may be taught, not so much with the expectation that it will prove eternally "true," but as a basis for learning the methodology of the field and as a basis for attacking the problems therein. Even the manipulative and motor skills assume some knowledge about the materials, methods, or tools that are used. Further, in another sense, all of the affective classifications make use of or are based upon knowledge. Thus, it is generally held that interests are developed as the result of an increase in information; likewise, attitudes and appreciations are regarded as having some base in knowledge or information. Even the objectives involving personal adjustment are quite frequently based upon the notion that a person must have some knowledge about himself before he can proceed to resolve his conflicts, anxieties, or other individual difficulties. It is clear that justification of knowledge for all these uses will usually involve knowledge in relation to other objectives, rather than knowledge for its own sake.

Still another justification for the development of knowledge as an objective of education arises from the status of knowledge in our own culture. Many workers assume a positive relationship between increase in knowledge and increase in maturity. In fact, quite frequently the increasing maturity of individuals or groups is judged in terms of their increasing knowledge about themselves or about the world in which they live. Knowledge is also frequently regarded as an important criterion of brightness or intelligence. This is reflected in intelligence testing where vocabulary or knowledge questions predominate and are regarded as signs of intelligence. In many schools, knowledge is regarded as the primary index of the level of education an individual has attained. This is indicated by the content of our standardized achievement test. The layman frequently regards knowledge and education as being synonymous. The great emphasis on radio quiz programs and tests of either historical or contemporary information which appear in newspapers and magazines further reflects the status of knowledge in our culture. There is little doubt that our culture places tremendous weight on knowledge or information as an important characteristic of the individual.

Many teachers and educators prize knowledge to some extent because of the simplicity with which it can be taught or learned. Mass methods, such as lectures, audio-visual methods, printed material,and the like, can be readily used for the acquisition of information. Quite frequently we tend to think of knowledge as something which is learned as the result of simply presenting it to the learner in one form of communication or another. Clearly related to this is the ease with which it is possible to gauge the extent to which the student has acquired knowledge. Practically all teachers have considerable confidence in their ability to build tests of knowledge. Because of the simplicity of teaching and evaluating knowledge, it is frequently emphasized as an educational objective out of all proportion to its usefulness or its relevance for the development of the individual. In effect, the teacher and school tend to look where the light is brightest and where it is least difficult to develop the individual.

Requiring that a student learn certain knowledge assumes a prediction that the student is likely to be able to make some use of the knowledge in the future. Thus, knowledge about phenomena relevant to the specialization of the engineer is maximally useful if the student is to become an engineer. Requiring the student to learn about engineering phenomena means that we can predict that he will be an engineer or that the knowledge will transfer to other areas where he is likely to be able to use it. Knowledge required of students prior to their making a firm vocational choice will need to have more general relevance and widespread usefulness than after a firm choice is made. Extensive knowledge requirements in rapidly changing specialized fields need to be checked against the best possible prediction of what knowledge will be of continuing use and what knowledge is necessary for a grasp of the current known field. The teacher and the curriculum specialist must take all these factors into account in determining what knowledge to select.

Undoubtedly the greatest predictability arises within the school itself where it may be known that the knowledge learned in one class will be used in one way or another in a subsequent course. Conversely, there is least predictability in the attempt to relate what is learned in the classroom to what the student may need as a citizen or specialist.

Our general understanding of learning theory would seem to indicate that knowledge which is organized and related is better learned and retained than knowledge which is specific and isolated. By this we mean that learning a large number of isolated specifics is quite difficult simply because of the multiplicity of items to be remembered. Further, they cannot be retained very well if they are kept in such isolation. Thus one hundred nonsense syllables would be more difficult to learn than an equal number of syllables in a meaningful poem. Specifics can be learned in relation to a general abstraction, and as a result can be remembered or retained best in this relationship. When learning takes place in this way, it is possible for an individual who remembers the generalization to proceed relatively easily to some of the specifics subsumed under that generalization.

On the other hand, generalizations or abstractions are relatively difficult to learn unless they are related to appropriate concrete phenomena. A generalization isolated from the phenomena it covers is very difficult to learn and very hard to retain. As a matter of fact, some definitions of intelligence[7] regard the abstractness of the ideas an individual can understand as a good index of the level of intelligence.

Curricular decisions to be made about knowledge objectives

Four decisions to be made with respect to the nature of the knowledge objectives included in the curriculum should be noted. These relate to "How much knowledge should be required learning?"; "How precisely need the student learn the required knowledge?"; "How is knowledge best organized for learning?"; and "How meaningful need required knowledge-learning be to the student?"

Decisions with respect to "How much knowledge should be required learning?" must strike a balance between attempts to include all the knowledge the individual might conceivably acquire in a particular subject and only that knowledge which is most basic to the subject. Rarely does the educator lean toward the latter of these two alternatives. Some educators frequently assume that the knowledge which the expert or specialist needs to possess about a field or topic and the knowledge which the beginning student may reasonably be expected to learn are identical. Such an assumption tends to overestimate the student's ability to learn and retain information. These educators must decide whether the student's time and effort are best used in becoming acquainted with the major knowledge in the field or in thoroughly mastering that knowledge which is basic to further learning in the field. For instance, in the field of mathematics it would be possible for the student to become aware of the existence and nature of the major mathematical techniques or to concentrate on learning the fundamentals which would permit him to later pick up these techniques on his own.

[7] See Stoddard, George D., The Meaning of Intelligence, New York: The Macmillan Co., 1944.

A second decision, the degree of precision to be required of the student, is not unrelated to the first. Thus, requiring the student to "become aware of the existence and nature of the major mathematical techniques" would presumably permit the student some latitude in the precision of his recall of the details of the techniques. On the other hand, to "thoroughly master that mathematical knowledge which is basic to further learning" implies a rather high standard of precision in the learning of this material. This decision about the precision to be required of the student exists at all levels of knowledge. Thus, even in the simplest type of objective such as knowledge of terminology, it is quite conceivable for a student to learn definitions of terms at many different levels of accuracy and precision. Usually greater precision is required at later stages of training. Thus, the student is introduced to an item of knowledge at a general but accurate level, gradually making finer and finer distinctions as he uses the item until he has reached the more detailed and precise level of the expert.

A third decision relates to the best organization of knowledge to facilitate learning. As previously noted, the cases of the specialist and the student are not identical. The organization the specialist finds most useful is not necessarily the organization that provides the easiest learning path for the student. The decision to be made is whether to use an organization externally imposed by some authority or expert as compared with an organization that fits the internal state of the learner at his particular stage of development.

A fourth decision with respect to the nature of knowledge objectives in the curriculum relates to the immediate as opposed to the future need of the student for this information. A student can memorize a body of information whether or not he finds immediate use for it or whether it meets any of his present needs. This is particularly true once the student becomes habituated to this kind of learning, as many of our students have. Many schools orient their students in this direction by the use of grades, examinations, and competition. It is likely that if the teacher believes the learning of knowledge is important or can communicate the importance of it to the students, there will be little difficulty in obtaining learning of even the most artificial and esoteric kinds of information.

The nature of abilities and skills

Although information or knowledge is recognized as an important outcome of education, very few teachers would be satisfied to regard this as the primary or the sole outcome of instruction. What is needed is some evidence that the students can do something with their knowledge, that is, that they can apply the information to new situations and problems. It is also expected that students will acquire generalized techniques for dealing with new problems and new materials. Thus, it is expected that when the student encounters a new problem or situation, he will select an appropriate technique for attacking it and will bring to bear the necessary information, both facts and principles. This has been labeled "critical thinking" by some, "reflective thinking" by Dewey and others, and "problem solving" by still others. In the taxonomy we have used the term "intellectual abilities and skills." The most general operational definition of these abilities and skills is that the individual can find appropriate information and techniques in his previous experience to bring to bear on new problems and situations. This requires some analysis or understanding of the new situation; it requires a background of knowledge or methods which can be readily utilized; and it also requires some facility in discerning the appropriate relations between previous experience and the new situation.

Arts or skills + knowledge = abilities

Sometimes in educational achievement testing we wish to distinguish between what we might call "intellectual abilities" and "intellectual arts and skills." "Arts and skills" refer to modes of operation and generalized techniques for dealing with problems. In testing for arts and skills, the problems and materials are of such a nature that little or no specialized and technical information is required. Whatever information is required is assumed to be part of the general fund of knowledge of the group being tested. The emphasis in testing is on the examinee's competence in using a generalized method of operating or dealing with a new problem situation. The arts and skills emphasize the mental processes of organizing and reorganizing material to achieve a particular purpose.

The intellectual abilities, on the other hand, refer to situations in which the individual is expected to bring specific technical information to bear on a new problem. They represent combinations of knowledge and intellectual arts and skills. In solving problems requiring intellectual abilities, the student is expected to organize or reorganize a problem, to recognize what material is appropriate, to remember such material, and to make use of it in the problem situation. In the case both of abilities and of skills, the problems are intended to be new and unfamiliar to the student.

Although this distinction between intellectual abilities and intellectual skills may be made in achievement testing, it is rather difficult to classify educational objectives and test items as abilities or skills without a full knowledge of the prior experience of the students. It is for this reason that the distinction has been omitted in the taxonomy and is only briefly mentioned here.

Justification for the development of intellectual abilities and skills

Justification for the development of intellectual abilities and skills can readily be derived from a consideration of the nature of the society and culture in which we live, the knowledge that is available to us, and the kind of citizen the schools seek to develop. Further justification may be derived from what is known in educational psychology about the permanence of various kinds of learning and the extent to which various kinds of learning can be transferred to new situations.

The development of problem-solving skills (intellectual abilities and skills) is not equally necessary in all societies and cultures. It is possible to imagine a society or culture which is relatively fixed. Such a society represents a closed system in which it is possible to predict in advance both the kinds of problems individuals will encounter and the solutions which are appropriate to those problems. Where such predictions can be made in advance, it is possible to organize the educational experiences so as to give each individual the particular knowledge and the specific methods needed for solving the problems he will encounter. Probably the nearest one can come to such a closed system in our culture is in some aspects of military life. For instance, if one is training an individual to be a radio technician for military work, it is frequently possible to know in advance exactly what kind of radio circuits he will have to work with. Under these conditions it is possible to reduce the amount of training to only these particular radio circuits and to teach the individual how to solve all the foreseeable difficulties he will encounter in working with them. Such training can be quick and efficient, but it is highly restricted since it is applicable to only a very limited range of situations.

Whatever the case in the past, it is very clear that in the middle of the 20th century we find ourselves in a rapidly changing and unpredictable culture. It seems almost impossible to foresee the particular ways in which it will change in the near future or the particular problems which will be paramount in five or ten years. Under these conditions, much emphasis must be placed in the schools on the development of generalized ways of attacking problems and on knowledge which can be applied to a wide range of new situations. That is, we have the task of preparing individuals for problems that cannot be foreseen in advance, and about all that can be done under such conditions is to help the student acquire generalized intellectual abilities and skills which will serve him well in many new situations. This places faith in the intellectual virtues as providing some form of stability for the individual who must find or make some order in his world.

However, even in the relatively stable culture or society, we do have to recognize that all knowledge is partial and that each situation the individual encounters has some unique characteristics. Forced to act, the individual has the task of taking what knowledge he has (which is only partially appropriate to a situation) and determining its relevance to the new situation. Since each situation is unique, the individual must be able to recognize which essential characteristics of the new situation are related to situations he has already encountered; then he must apply the correct knowledge and method with appropriate modifications. Clearly it is impossible to give the individual all the knowledge he will ever need for every new situation he will encounter. It is possible, however, to help him acquire that knowledge which has been found most useful in the past, and to help him develop those intellectual abilities and skills which will enable him to adapt that knowledge to the new situations.

The importance of the intellectual abilities and skills is further illustrated by our recognition of the individual's ability to independently attack his problems as a desirable sign of maturity. Individuals are expected, as they mature, to solve problems on their own and to make decisions wisely on the basis of their own thinking. Further, this independent problem solving is regarded as one indication of the individual's adjustment. It is recognized that unless the individual can do his own problem solving he cannot maintain his integrity as an independent personality.

Closely allied to this concept of maturity and integrity is the concept of the individual as a member of a democracy. Citizens are expected to make important and independent decisions about governmental problems and about their political future. It is clear that many of these decisions require problem solving of a very high order. It is impossible to tell an individual in advance how to vote or even the bases on which he should vote. These are matters he must decide repeatedly throughout his life whenever a major election takes place. But more than specific elections and voting is the concept of individuals in a democracy as independent decision-makers who, in the last analysis, are responsible for the conduct of a democratic political system as well as a democratic way of life.

The above justifications for the development of intellectual abilities and skills reflect a number of value components in relation to the concept of the good life. The following two reasons have to do primarily with the efficiency of the learning process.

As we have defined intellectual abilities and skills, they are more widely applicable than knowledge. If we are concerned with the problem of transfer of training, by definition we would select intellectual abilities and skills as having greater transfer value.

A second reason for the efficiency of intellectual abilities and skills in learning is their permanence. From psychological theory (e. g., reinforcement theory) it would seem reasonable to expect greater permanence of learning for those outcomes of education which can be generalized and applied in a number of different situations throughout the individual's formal educational experience than for those outcomes which are so specific that they are likely to be encountered only once or at the most a few times throughout the educational program. It would seem desirable to determine whether research evidence is in support of our logical and pedagogical distinctions. While only a few studies in the literature deal with this problem, the findings are in general support of the foregoing. [8,9,10]

Finally, the foregoing discussion has illustrated the importance of the abilities and skills for both the individual and his society, and it has noted the learning efficiency of the abilities and skills. But common observation would indicate that individuals in general tend to avoid real problem solving. When presented with problems, they usually apply a limited stock of techniques to them and are frequently satisfied if a partial solution is obtained. If the techniques

[8] Freud, H., and Cheronis, N. D., "Retention in the Physical Science Survey Course," Journal of Chemical Education, 17 (1940), pp. 289-93.

[9] Frutchey, F. P., "Retention in High School Chemistry," Journal of Higher Education, 8 (1937), pp. 217-18.

[10] Tyler, R. W., "Permanence of Learning," in Constructing Achievement Tests, Columbus: Ohio State University, 1934.

do not work, there is a strong tendency either to reorder the problem completely (that is, to make it a new problem) or to escape from it entirely. Rarely do individuals stay with a difficult problem for any considerable length of time and try increasingly varied procedures for attacking it. Yet, we need more than ever to help students develop problem-solving methods which will yield more complete and adequate solutions in a wide range of problem situations. It is to be hoped that the taxonomy's analysis of this area will facilitate the exploration of new methods of teaching for high-level problem solving and assist in evaluating these methods.

CHAPTER 3

THE PROBLEMS OF CLASSIFYING
EDUCATIONAL OBJECTIVES
AND TEST EXERCISES

Three levels of definition in each taxonomy category

The taxonomy Handbook in its present form defines a class or sub-class of educational objectives in three ways. The first and major type of definition is represented by a verbal description or definition of each class and sub-class. The exact phrasing of these definitions has been the subject of much debate among us and, while the present definitions are far from ideal, every effort has been made to describe the major aspects of each category as carefully as possible.

A second type of definition is provided by the list of educational objectives which are included under each sub-class of the taxonomy. The objectives used here have been selected from the published literature on curriculum and testing as well as from unpublished materials available in the files of the examiners and curriculum specialists. In a number of cases, the objectives have been slightly modified in order to more precisely express the student behavior intended. Most of the objectives listed in this Handbook have been selected from courses and programs at the general education and secondary education levels. While some attempt has been made to select objectives from different subject fields, it is likely that each subject is not equally well represented in these lists. Inclusion of an objective in this volume does not mean that we believe it is an important objective or even that it is the best way of formulating such an objective. We do believe that the objectives finally included are representative of those found in the literature and that they are appropriately classified.

The third type of definition attempts to make clear the behavior appropriate to each category by illustrations of the examination questions and problems which are regarded as appropriate. In a way, this represents the most detailed and precise definition of the sub-class since it indicates the tasks the student is expected to perform and the specific behavior he is expected to exhibit. The illustrative test exercises included in this Handbook have been selected from published examinations as well as from examinations available in the files of the cooperating examiners. While some effort has been made to draw these examples from the different subject fields and from secondary as well as college courses, it is likely that particular areas and particular levels are not as fully illustrated as desirable. The reader will note the high proportion of so called "objective" or recognition forms of test questions. This does not reflect a bias against carefully devised essay or other types of test situations. We have made use of illustrations which were readily available and selected examples which most clearly illustrated the category.

In order to help the reader get an over-all view of the taxonomy and to help him in its use, we have printed a condensed version of the taxonomy in the Appendix. Each of the classes of objectives is defined in greater detail in the appropriate section of this volume where it is accompanied by a discussion of the particular objectives and test illustrations which are relevant.

The classification of objectives

To help the reader in making use of the taxonomy, this chapter is devoted to a discussion of the problems of classifying educational objectives and test exercises. A number of illustrative objectives and test exercises are provided for the reader to classify for himself. He can then compare his classification with those made by the writers. The intent of this chapter is thus to bring the reader closer to the taxonomy and to convert it from an empty set of terms and definitions to one that the reader finds workable and applicable to his own situation.

We begin by selecting three objectives from Volume I of Higher Education for American Democracy[1] which appear to be relevant to the cognitive domain of the taxonomy.

---

[1] A Report of the President's Commission on Higher Education. Higher Education for American Democracy, Volume I, Establishing the Goals. U. S. Government Printing Office, Washington, December, 1947.

(A) to understand the ideas of others and to express one's own effectively (p. 52)

(B) to acquire the knowledge (and attitudes) basic to a satisfying family life (p. 56)

(C) to acquire and use the skills and habits involved in critical and constructive thinking (p. 57)

All three of these would appear to represent desirable outcomes of learning. However, they are such broad objectives that the kinds of learning experiences which might be appropriate are far from clear. At this level of generality one would also have great difficulty in determining the types of evaluation evidence which could reveal whether or not students have actually developed the necessary competence. As they are stated, these broad objectives could only be classified under such broad categories as knowledge or intellectual abilities. Thus, objective A includes both understanding of ideas and (the ability) to express ideas effectively. At this level of generality the objective could be included under each of the six major categories of this taxonomy. Objective C quite clearly goes beyond the knowledge category, but it could quite properly be included under each of the remaining five categories of Comprehension, Application, Analysis, Synthesis, and Evaluation. Objective B includes both knowledge and attitudes. However, if only the knowledge aspect of this objective is considered, it could quite properly be classified under category 1.00 of this taxonomy—Knowledge. It is, however, impossible to determine which of the different subclasses of knowledge are appropriate.

The user of the taxonomy will find that, all too frequently, educational objectives are stated so broadly that little can be done with them for curricular or evaluation purposes until they have been more adequately defined. As broad outcomes they are extremely useful in suggesting general policy for a particular educational institution, for a group of institutions, or for a type of educational program. And, in fact, this level of generality is typical of college catalogs and the printed statements of aims of secondary schools. The majority of publications in which some educational policy group or general curriculum group attempts to define or suggest the desired outcomes of education are couched in terms equally broad. When faculty groups first begin to state their educational objectives they tend to make use of aims stated as generally as those found in the report of the President's Commission on Higher Education. Although the taxonomy is not too useful in classifying such broadly stated outcomes of learning, it is useful in helping to determine the level of specificity at which statements of objectives can be utilized in planning learning experiences and suggesting types of evaluation evidence which might be appropriate. The taxonomy is also useful as a means of raising questions which can have the effect of more clearly defining such generalized outcomes. All this is to say that the reader should not be overly frustrated at encountering and attempting to deal with educational objectives which are so broad that little can be done with them as far as classification is concerned. He should also recognize that at this level of generality little can be done with them as far as specific problems of curriculum and evaluation are concerned. Nevertheless, it is repeated that such broad aims are useful in pointing up general policy and directions for curriculum development.

A somewhat more clearly defined set of educational objectives for purposes of illustration is offered by the report "A Design for General Education."[2] This report, like the President's Commission report on Higher Education, has a list of broad outcomes of general education. Three of them which are parallel to those reported on page 46 are:

(D) to communicate through his own language in writing and speaking at the level of expression adequate to the needs of educated people (p. 14)

(E) to think through the problems and to gain the basic orientation that will better enable him to make a satisfactory family and marital adjustment (p. 14)

(F) to act in the light of an understanding of the natural phenomena in his environment in its implications for

[2] American Council on Education Studies. "A Design for General Education," American Council on Education, Washington, June 1944.

human society and human welfare, to use scientific
methods in the solution of his problems, and to employ useful nonverbal methods of thought and communication (p. 14)

These are obviously too broad to classify with any precision
in the taxonomy. However, in addition to these broad outcomes, the Design includes over 200 objectives which are
more clearly defined in terms of student behavior and subject matter content. These more specific objectives are
grouped under ten broad outcomes. The specific objectives can be classified with some precision under the appropriate categories and sub-categories of the cognitive domain.
Five of these are selected for purposes of discussion.

(G) (Knowledge and understanding) of reliable
sources of information on health (p. 31)

Although the full intent of the word "understanding" is not
clear, the emphasis on knowing, and possibly remembering,
places this objective rather clearly under the general heading of 1.00 Knowledge. Since the emphasis appears to be on
the knowledge of reliable sources rather than on the ability
to locate new sources or the ability to analyze the accuracy
and reliability of sources, this objective is classifiable as
1.12 Knowledge of specific facts.

(H) To read significant writings with critical
comprehension (p. 34)

Although the full intent of the word "critical" is not
clear, the emphasis on reading and comprehension suggests
that this objective is appropriately classified under the major
category, 2.00 Comprehension. Although a case could be
made for including this objective under 2.10 Translation or
2.30 Extrapolation, it is likely that the objective is more
accurately classified as 2.20 Interpretation, since this is
the sub-category of Comprehension which emphasizes the
grasping of the meaning of a written work.

(I) The ability to apply principles to new
situations (p. 43)

This objective is described in such a way as to apply
most directly to category 3.00 Application.

(J)　The ability to recognize form and pattern in literary works as a means of understanding their meaning (p. 44)

This objective apparently involves a competence in analyzing the organization of a literary work to determine its formal and structural characteristics. This type of skill is included under the category 4.00 Analysis. Since it can be defined as involving an analysis of the structure and organization of a communication, it is appropriately classified under 4.30 Analysis of organizational principles.

(K)　The ability to select and organize ideas and experiences with reference to socially desirable purposes of communication (p. 33)

In this objective the emphasis appears to be on the putting together of elements and parts so as to form a whole. As such it would be an example of what we have termed 5.00 Synthesis. It can further be defined as the first subcategory of synthesis, 5.10 Production of a unique communication, since for the individual writer or speaker the emphasis is on the communication, rather than on the other types of synthesis defined under this major category.

(L)　The ability to identify and appraise judgments and values that are involved in the choice of a course of action (p. 41)

The identification of the judgments and values involved in the choice of a course of action suggests a type of comprehension or analysis. However, the appraisal of the judgment and values represents a kind of evaluation. The rule we have adopted is to place the objective under the highest type of classification (the most complex) which is appropriate. Therefore, this objective would be classified as 6.00 Evaluation. Since the evaluation of judgments and values must, if it is to be based on cognitive grounds, refer to some sort of external criteria, the appropriate classification of this objective is 6.20 Judgments in terms of external criteria.

Test yourself on the classification of objectives

The reader may wish to try his hand at classifying other objectives under the categories of the condensed version of the taxonomy in the Appendix. For this purpose the following 10 objectives have been selected from "A Design for General Education." The Key to the classification of each of these objectives will be found on page 59.

1. (Knowledge) of community organizations and services for health maintenance and improvement (p. 31)

2. (Knowledge) of acceptable usage in articulation, pronunciation, capitalization, grammar, and spelling as a means of effective presentation (p. 33)

3. (Ability) to listen to important oral statements with concentration and judgment (p. 34)

4. (Knowledge) of the criteria of normal and neurotic adjustment (p. 35)

5. (Knowledge) of the trends in American society affecting the structure and functions of the family and the role of women and children in our society (p. 36)

6. The ability to read graphs, diagrams, and blueprints (p. 43)

7. (Knowledge) of the techniques and methods used by scientists in seeking to answer questions about the world, and of the proper functions of scientific theory and experiment (p. 42)

8. The ability to recognize artistic quality in contemporary works of music and art (p. 45)

9. The ability to formulate explicitly and systematically a pattern of values as a basis of individual and social action (p. 41)

10. The ability to evaluate popular health beliefs critically (p. 32)

The problems of classifying test exercises

The task of classifying test exercises is somewhat more complicated than that of classifying educational objectives. Before the reader can classify a particular test exercise he must know, or at least make some assumptions about, the learning situations which have preceded the test. He must also actually attempt to solve the test problem and note the mental processes he utilizes. The reader should also take into consideration the possibility that the processes used in selecting the correct answer in a recognition form of question may be somewhat different from those used in considering the incorrect alternatives in the same question. For purposes of illustration we have selected a series of test exercises from the book, The Measurement of Understanding. [3]

(I)   As the number of mechanical inventions increases and society becomes more complex: (1) Each worker does more specialized work. (2) Each person takes care directly of more of his needs. (3) People depend less on each other. (4) Each worker does a greater variety of work. (p. 88)

It is assumed that the student has had learning experiences which stress specialization of function with increasing industrialization and complexity of the society. Although the particular formulation of the test item may be new, the concept of specialization is familiar. With this assumption, the item is clearly classified under 1.00 Knowledge. Since the emphasis is on a generalized concept rather than particular concrete facts, it is appropriate to further classify it under the sub-category 1.31 Knowledge of principles and generalizations.

(II)   From which could you obtain information concerning the location of the principal oil fields of the United States? (1) Department of State (2) Department of Interior (3) Department of Education (4) Department of Agriculture (p. 91)

---

[3] Brownell, William A., Chairman, et al. The Measurement of Understanding, The Forty-fifth Yearbook of the National Society for the Study of Education, Part I, Chicago: The University of Chicago Press, March 1946.

It is assumed that the student has learned about the functions of the different departments and that he has learned about the types of publications and kinds of information one might in general secure from each department. This would then be readily classified under 1.00 Knowledge. Since what is asked for is a relatively detailed bit of information, it would be further classified as 1.12 Knowledge of specific facts.

(III) The underlined statement at the end of the problem is assumed to be a correct answer. You are to explain the underlined conclusion by selecting statements from the list following the problem. (The student checks the explanations.)

If a person is planning to bathe in the sun, at what time of day is he most likely to receive a severe sunburn? He is most likely to receive a severe sunburn in the middle of the day (11 A.M. to 1 P.M.) because:

_____ We are slightly closer to the sun at noon than in the morning or afternoon.

_____ The noon sun will produce more "burn" than the morning or afternoon sun.

_____ When the sun's rays fall directly (straight down) on a surface, more energy is received by that surface than when the rays fall obliquely on the surface.

_____ When the sun's rays fall directly (straight down) on a surface, less sunshine is reflected from the surface than when the sun's rays fall obliquely on that surface.

_____ When the sun is directly overhead the sun's rays pass through less absorbing atmosphere than when the sun is lower in the sky.

_____ Just as a bullet shot straight into a block of wood penetrates farther into the wood, so will the direct rays at noon penetrate more deeply into the skin.

_____ The air is usually warmer at noon than at other times of the day.

_____ The ultraviolet of the sunlight is mainly responsible for sunburn. (114)

It is assumed that this is a new problem for the student and that the task is one of selecting the correct explanatory principle. Some of the alternatives offered are factually correct while others are incorrect. Some are relevant, others are irrelevant. Some merely repeat the conclusion, while others state the generalizations or principles which have explanatory value. Selecting the appropriate explanatory generalizations requires that the student be able to relate the appropriate generalizations to the situation. This would then be classified as 3.00 Application.

(IV) Statement of facts:

Family Income	Per Cent of Family Members Who Received No Medical Attention During the Year
Under $1200	47
$1200 to $3000	40
$3000 to $5000	33
$5000 to $10,000	24
Over $10,000	14

Conclusion: Members of families with small incomes are healthier than members with large incomes.

The conclusion is not completely justified by the facts given. It may be justified, however, if an assumption is made; that is, if a factor not stated in the given facts is taken for granted. What is this factor? That is, what must be assumed in addition to the facts given in order that the conclusion be true? (p. 127)

If it is assumed that the data and the problem are essentially new to the student, it requires that the student be able to identify the assumption which must be made to support the conclusion in relation to the data. It is thus an example of 4.10 Analysis of elements.

(V) A 6A class was studying the geography of Europe and the land of the Dutch people. Someone in the class said that the homes of the Dutch people who live in America are always neat and clean. The teacher asked this question, "What reasons can you give for thinking that they are always neat and clean?"

Here are some of the reasons the children gave. Read them carefully and decide which are the best and which are the poorest.

_____ I heard someone say that they were neat and clean.

_____ I was in one Dutch home and it was clean.

_____ Our geography book said they were clean.

_____ I have been in many Dutch homes and all of them were neat and clean.

_____ I read in the story book that these houses were always neat and clean. (p. 93)

Here the student is expected to judge the value of reasons in relation to a new question which is posed in the problem. It is clearly an example of 6.00 Evaluation. Since the emphasis is on quality of evidence in relation to the sources and the comprehensiveness of the information it could appropriately be placed under the sub-category of 6.20 Judgments in terms of external criteria.

Test yourself on the classification of test exercises

The reader may now wish to try his hand at classifying additional test exercises. The following exercises have been selected from the book, Measurement of Understanding. The key to the classification of these exercises will be found on page 59.

In the following problem, assume that the student has studied tariffs in some detail.

_____ 1. Which has been a result of this country's policy of maintaining a high protective tariff? (1) Higher prices for domestic goods (2) lower prices for foreign goods (3) increased foreign trade (4) higher prices for farm products sold in foreign markets (p. 88)

- - - - - -

Assume that the data in the following exercise are new to the student.

The table below shows the combined expenditures of all state governments in the United States for various governmental services. Amounts are in thousands of dollars.

	1910		1920		1930	
	Amount	Per cent of total	Amount	Per cent of total	Amount	Per cent of total
1. General government expenses	$ 43,400	11.7	$ 74,053	10.5	$ 125,000	9.1
2. Protection	19,425	5.3	32,000	4.6	72,000	5.4
3. Health	20,302	5.4	28,475	4.2	41,450	3.1
4. Recreation	2,162	0.5	4,820	0.6	9,512	0.7
5. Highways	58,300	15.9	125,400	18.2	292,441	21.3
6. Welfare	86,621	23.4	121,850	17.6	214,500	15.1
7. Education	148,265	37.8	315,122	44.3	591,240	45.3
	$378,475	100.0	$701,720	100.0	$1,346,143	100.0

For the purpose of checking the statements at the end of this problem, the data alone:

(1) are sufficient to make the statement true.
(2) are sufficient to indicate that the statement is probably true.
(3) are not sufficient to indicate whether there is any degree of truth or falsity in the statement.
(4) are sufficient to indicate that the statement is probably false.
(5) are sufficient to make the statement false.

Mark each of the following statements with the number of one of the foregoing statements which indicates your interpretation of the data in the table.

2. _____ In 1935 less was spent for general government expenses than for highways.
3. _____ The highway expenditures of New York, Ohio, and Illinois together were at least twice as large in 1930 as in 1910.
4. _____ In 1930 more than five times as much money was spent for highways as for health.
5. _____ In 1929 at least 35 per cent of the total expenditures of the states was for education.
6. _____ The expenditures for each type of service shown in the table increased between 1910 and 1930. (p. 94)

- - - - -

Assume that the student has learned something about meteorology, but that the particular relationships between the fact and the statements have not been studied in this form.

7. Tell whether each of the statements following the fact is (A) a cause of the fact, (B) a result of the fact, or (C) not related to the fact.

Fact: A flash of lightning occurs.

Statements

A roar of thunder can be heard.   _____

Electricity passed between clouds and the earth.   _____

It is dangerous to stand under a tree during a
rainstorm.   (p. 135)   _____

Some additional test exercises drawn from the files of the cooperating examiners are presented below.

8. A brick can be pulled along a fairly smooth surface by means of a string; the string would break, however, if jerked sharply. Which of the following principles is most directly useful in explaining this fact?

>   A- Force is equal to mass times acceleration.
>   B- Friction exists between any two bodies in contact with each other.
>   C- Conservation of momentum
>   D- Conservation of energy
>   E- None of these principles applies.

- - - - - -

"For what men say is that, if I am really just and am not also thought just, profit there is none, but the pain and loss on the other hand are unmistakable. But if, though unjust, I acquire the reputation of justice, a heavenly life is promised to me. Since then appearance tyrannizes over truth and is lord of happiness, to appearance I must devote myself. I will describe around me a picture and shadow of virtue to be the vestibule and exterior of my house; behind I will trail the subtle and crafty fox."

9. Which one of the following best expresses the main topic of this selection?

>   A- What is justice?
>   B- How to attain eternal life
>   C- How to be successful
>   D- What is the nature of virtue?
>   E- What is truth?

10. Which of the following might be most inclined to follow the policy recommended in the selection?

>   A- An absolute ruler
>   B- A politician
>   C- A philosopher
>   D- A statesman
>   E- A religious leader

- - - - - -

11. If some external force should shift the earth nearer the sun so that the mean radius of its orbit would be eighty million miles, the anticipated effect on the earth would cause the

    A- seasons to be longer.
    B- sidereal day to be longer.
    C- average yearly temperature to be lower.
    D- year to be shorter.
    E- None of these.

12. Which one of the following actions would probably be least effective in correcting the undesirable features of group political pressures?

    A- Overhaul the national patent system.
    B- Concentrate the economic power of the nation.
    C- Give the public more information about the origin and extent of political lobbying.
    D- Use congressional investigating committees.
    E- Encourage all groups to subordinate their interests to the national interest.

13. Set the following poem to music:

_____ by_____
(Copy furnished the student)

Write a simple melodic line.

Write a composition with a single tonal base.

Write a composition using two tonal levels.

Write a specific work in a larger form for any of the accepted mediums of expression such as a chamber group, orchestra, chorus, or piano. The composition should be at least ten minutes' duration and have received performance. Suggested designs are as follows: a string quartet, a trio, or a sonata for violin or violincello and piano, or a work for full orchestra, or a dramatic work or a cantata for solos, chorus, and orchestra of at least fifteen minutes' duration. (Thesis requirement for master's degree in music.)

Key to the Classification
of Educational Objectives

Objective		Classification
1	. . . .	1.12
2	. . . .	1.21
3	. . . .	2.00, and perhaps 2.20
4	. . . .	1.24
5	. . . .	1.22
6	. . . .	2.10
7	. . . .	1.25
8	. . . .	4.30 or 6.20
9	. . . .	5.20
10	. . . .	6.20

Key to the Classification
of Test Exercises

Test Exercise		Classification
1	. . . .	1.22
2	. . . .	2.30
3	. . . .	2.30
4	. . . .	2.10
5	. . . .	2.30
6	. . . .	2.10
7	. . . .	4.20
8	. . . .	1.31
9	. . . .	2.20
10	. . . .	2.30
11	. . . .	3.00
12	. . . .	6.20
13	. . . .	5.10

PART II

THE TAXONOMY

AND

ILLUSTRATIVE MATERIALS

1.00 KNOWLEDGE

Knowledge as defined here includes those behaviors and
test situations which emphasize the remembering, either by
recognition or recall, of ideas, material, or phenomena.
The behavior expected of a student in the recall situation is
very similar to the behavior he was expected to have during
the original learning situation. In the learning situation the
student is expected to store in his mind certain information,
and the behavior expected later is the remembering of this
information. Although some alterations may be expected in
the material to be remembered, this is a relatively minor
part of the knowledge behavior or test. The process of relating and judging is also involved to the extent that the student is expected to answer questions or problems which are
posed in a different form in the test situation than in the
original learning situation.

In the classification of the knowledge objectives, the arrangement is from the specific and relatively concrete types
of behaviors to the more complex and abstract ones. Thus,
the knowledge of specifics refers to types of information or
knowledge which can be isolated and remembered separately,
while the knowledge of universals and abstractions emphasizes the interrelations and patterns in which information can
be organized and structured.

While it is recognized that knowledge is involved in the
more complex major categories of the taxonomy (2.00 to
6.00), the knowledge category differs from the others in that
remembering is the major psychological process involved
here, while in the other categories the remembering is only
one part of a much more complex process of relating, judging, and reorganizing.

1.10 KNOWLEDGE OF SPECIFICS

The recall of specific and isolable bits of information. --
This refers primarily to what might be called the hard core
of facts or information in each field of knowledge. Such information represents the elements the specialist must use in
communicating about his field, in understanding it, and in organizing it systematically. These specifics are usually quite
serviceable to people working in the field in the very form
in which they are presented and need little or no alteration
from one use or application to another. Such specifics also
become the basic elements the student or learner must know
if he is to be acquainted with the field or to solve any of the
problems in it. These specifics usually are symbols which
have some concrete referents and are, for the most part, at
a relatively low level of abstraction. There is a tremendous
wealth of these specifics and there must always be some selection for educational purposes, since it is almost inconceiv-
able that a student can learn all of the specifics relevant to a
particular field. As our knowledge in the social sciences,
the sciences, and the humanities increases, even the specialist has great difficulty in keeping up with all the new specifics
found or developed in the field. For classification purposes,
the specifics may be distinguished from the more complex
classes of knowledge by virtue of their very specificity, that
is, they can be isolated as elements or bits which have some
meaning and value by themselves.

1.11 - Knowledge of terminology

Knowledge of the referents for specific verbal and non-
verbal symbols. -- This may include knowledge of the most
generally accepted symbol referent, knowledge of the variety
of symbols which may be used for a single referent, or knowledge of the referent most appropriate to a given use of a symbol.

Probably the most basic type of knowledge in a particular

field is its terminology. Each field contains a large number of symbols, either verbal or non-verbal, which have particular referents. These represent the basic language of the field--the shorthand used by the workers in a field to express what they know. In any attempt by workers to communicate with others about phenomena within the field, they find it necessary to make use of some of the special symbols and terms they have devised. In many cases it is impossible for them to discuss problems in their field without making use of some of the essential terms of that field. Quite literally, they are unable to even think about many of the phenomena in the field unless they make use of these terms and symbols. The learner must become cognizant of these terms and symbols and must learn the generally accepted definitions or meanings to be attached. Just as the specialist in the field must communicate by the use of these terms, so the learner or the individual reader of the communication must have a knowledge of the symbols and their referents before he can comprehend or think about the phenomena of the field.

Here, to a larger extent than in any of the other classes of knowledge objectives, there is a likelihood that the specialist, finding his own symbols useful and precise, will attempt to impose upon the learner a larger number of the symbols than the learner really needs, can learn, or will retain. Especially is this true in many of the sciences which attempt to use words and symbols with great precision and where the specialist finds it difficult to express the same ideas or discuss particular phenomena by the use of other symbols or by the use of other terms much more common to a lay population.

1.11 <u>Knowledge of Terminology</u>--Illustrative Educational Objectives

To define technical terms by giving their attributes, properties, or relations.

The ability to distinguish the referents for words and to establish the limits within which a biological term may have meaning.

Familiarity with a large number of words in their common range of meanings.

Knowledge of the vocabulary of the fine arts sufficient
to be able to read and converse intelligently.

To acquire an understanding of the vocabulary used in
quantitative thinking.

Knowledge of the terms and concepts peculiar to work
in science.

Knowledge of important accounting terms.

Mastery of the terms peculiar to work in science.

To acquire an understanding of the terminology associated with geometric figures on a plane.

1.12 - <u>Knowledge of Specific Facts</u>

<u>Knowledge of dates, events, persons, places, sources
of information, etc.</u> -- This may include very precise and specific information, such as the exact date of an event or the
exact magnitude of a phenomenon. It may also include approximate information, such as a time period in which an
event occurred or the general order of magnitude of a phenomenon. Knowledge of specific facts refers to those facts which
can be isolated as separate, discrete elements in contrast to
those which can only be known in a larger context.

In every field there are a large number of dates, events,
persons, places, findings, etc., known by the specialist
which represent findings or knowledge about the field. These
can be distinguished from the terminology in that the terminology generally represents the conventions or agreements
within a field, while the facts are more likely to represent
the findings which can be tested by other means than determining the unanimity of workers in the field or the agreements
they have made for purposes of communication. Such specific
facts also represent basic elements which the specialist must
use in presenting communications about the field and in thinking about specific problems or topics in the field. It should
also be recognized that this classification includes knowledge
about particular books, writing, and sources of information
on specific topics and problems. Thus, knowledge of a specific fact as well as knowledge of the source which deals with
the fact are both classifiable under this heading.

Again, there is usually a tremendous number of such specific facts and the teacher or curriculum specialist must make choices as to what is basic and what is only of secondary importance or of importance primarily to the specialist. The teacher is also confronted with the problem of level of precision with which different information must be known. Thus, quite frequently he may be content to have a student learn only the approximate magnitude of the phenomenon rather than its precise quantity or to learn an approximate time period rather than the precise date or time of a specific event. The teacher also has a considerable problem in determining whether many of the specific facts are such that the student can learn them whenever he really needs them, or whether they should be learned during and as part of an educational unit or course.

1.12 Knowledge of Specific Facts--Illustrative Educational Objectives

The recall of major facts about particular cultures.

The possession of a minimum knowledge about the organisms studied in the laboratory.

Knowledge of biological facts important to a systematic understanding of biological processes.

Recall and recognition of factual information about contemporary society.

Knowledge of practical biological facts important to health, citizenship, and other human needs.

Acquiring information about major natural resources.

Acquiring information about various important aspects of nutrition.

Recall and recognition of what is characteristic of particular periods.

Knowledge of physical and chemical properties of common elements and their compounds.

An acquaintance with the more significant names, places, and events in the news.

A knowledge of the reputation of a given author for presenting and interpreting facts on governmental problems.

Knowledge of reliable sources of information for wise purchasing.

1.20 KNOWLEDGE OF WAYS AND MEANS
OF DEALING WITH SPECIFICS

Knowledge of the ways of organizing, studying, judging, and criticizing ideas and phenomena. --This includes the methods of inquiry, the chronological sequences, and the standards of judgment within a field as well as the patterns of organization through which the areas of the fields themselves are determined and internally organized.

At a somewhat more abstract level than the specifics are the methods of organizing and dealing with them. Each subject field has a body of techniques, criteria, classifications, and forms which are used to discover specifics as well as to deal with them once they are discovered. These differ from the specifics in that they form the connecting links between specifics, the operations necessary to establish or deal with specifics, and the criteria by which specifics are judged and evaluated. It must be made clear that this class of behaviors is only a very limited one as used here. It does not involve actual use of the ways and means so much as it does a knowledge of their existence and possible use. The actual skills and abilities which involve their use are described in the 2.00 to 6.00 classes of the taxonomy.

Although it will frequently be found difficult to distinguish knowledge of ways and means from knowledge of specifics for purposes of classification, several characteristics will be useful in making these distinctions. Ways and means will refer to processes rather than products. They will indicate operations rather than the results of operations. They will include knowledge which is largely the result of agreement and convenience rather than the knowledge which is more directly a matter of observation, experimentation, and discovery. They will more commonly be reflections of how workers in the field think and attack problems rather than the results of such thought or problem solving.

Although this class does not differ greatly from 1.10 - Knowledge of Specifics, it appears likely that students will have greater difficulty in learning this knowledge because of its greater abstractness. Added difficulty may occur because many of the ways and means may represent relatively arbitrary and even artificial forms which are meaningful only to the specialist who recognizes their value as tools and techniques in his work.

1.21 - Knowledge of Conventions

Knowledge of characteristic ways of treating and presenting ideas and phenomena. — These are the usages, styles, and practices which are employed in a field because the workers find they suit their purposes or because they appear to suit the phenomena with which they deal. This may include such varied phenomena as conventional symbols used in map making and dictionaries, rules of social behavior, and rules, styles, or practices commonly employed in scholarly fields.

There are many conventions and rules which the workers in a field find extremely useful in dealing with the phenomena of a field. Although many such conventions may be retained because of habit and tradition rather than usefulness, at some point in time they were found to be especially significant in giving some structure to the phenomena. Generally these conventions will have an arbitrary existence since they were developed or retained because of general agreement or concurrence of workers in the field. They are usually true only as a matter of definition and practice rather than as a result of discovery or observation.

In some fields these conventions make up the largest proportion of the knowledge of the field. It is likely that students are more willing to accept and learn this type of knowledge in the early school years than in the later years of formal education.

1.21 Knowledge of Conventions--Illustrative Educational Objectives

Familiarity with the forms and conventions of the major types of works, e.g., verse, plays, scientific papers, etc.

To make pupils conscious of correct form and usage in speech and writing.

Knowledge of common rules of etiquette.

To develop a knowledge of acceptable forms of language.

Knowledge of the ways in which symbols are used to indicate the correct pronunciation of words.

Knowledge of the standard representational devices and symbols in maps and charts.

A knowledge of the rules of punctuation.

1.22 - Knowledge of Trends and Sequences

Knowledge of the processes, directions, and movements of phenomena with respect to time. --It includes trends as attempts to point up the interrelationship among a number of specific events which are separated by time. It also includes representations of processes which may involve time as well as causal interrelations of a series of specific events. Out of an almost infinite number of specific events, particular workers have selected those which they believe point to a trend or sequence. In this respect trends and sequences are those relationships and processes which have been selected or emphasized by the workers in the field. Many of the trends and sequences are difficult to communicate because they involve highly dynamic actions, processes, and movements which are not fully represented by static verbal, graphic, or symbolic forms.

Students may have difficulty in learning trends and sequences unless they are also familiar with the specifics on which such trends and sequences are based.

1.22 Knowledge of Trends and Sequences--Illustrative Educational Objectives

Understanding of the continuity and development of American culture as exemplified in American life.

Knowledge of the basic trends underlying the development of public assistance programs with particular reference to such programs as WPA, PWA, etc., developed during the depression.

Knowledge of trends in government in the United States during the last fifty years.

To develop a basic knowledge of the evolutionary development of man.

To develop a knowledge of effects of industrialization on the culture and international relations of a nation.

To know and describe the forces which determine and shape public policies.

To understand the increasing importance of administrative departments of the national government in formulating public policies.

To know how Greek civilization has affected the contemporary world.

To know how militarism and imperialism have been of causal importance for the world wars.

To develop a knowledge of how hereditary and environmental factors interrelate to influence the development of the individual.

A knowledge of the forces, past and present, which have made for the increasing interdependence of people all over the world.

1.23 - Knowledge of Classifications and Categories

Knowledge of the classes, sets, divisions, and arrangements which are regarded as fundamental or useful for a given subject field, purpose, argument, or problem. --As a subject field, problem, or topic becomes well developed, individuals working on it find it useful to develop classifications and categories which help to structure and systematize the phenomena. These classifications and categories are likely to have an arbitrary and artificial flavor to the student, although the specialist finds them useful and even fundamental for his work. The individual student is expected to know these classifications and to know when they are appropriate. However, under the present heading is included only knowledge of the classifications and categories, while the application of these to new problems is dealt with in other parts of the taxonomy.

1.23 <u>Knowledge of Classification and Categories</u>--Illustrative Educational Objectives

To recognize the area encompassed by various kinds of problems or materials.

Becoming familiar with a range of types of literature.

Knowledge of the features of various forms of business ownership.

1.24 - <u>Knowledge of Criteria</u>

<u>Knowledge of the criteria by which facts, principles, opinions, and conduct are tested or judged</u>. -- Here again is a systematization which is found useful by workers attacking the problems of a field. Students may be expected to make use of the criteria as well as to have a knowledge of them. The utilization of the criteria in actual problem situations will be found in <u>6.00 - Evaluation</u>. The criteria will vary markedly from field to field. They are likely to appear complex and abstract to students and to acquire meaning only as they are related to concrete situations and problems.

1.24 Knowledge of Criteria--Illustrative Educational Objectives

Familiarity with criteria for judgment appropriate to the type of work and the purpose for which it is read.

Knowledge of criteria for the evaluation of recreational activities.

Knowledge of the criteria by which a valid source of information in the social sciences can be recognized.

Knowledge of the criteria by which the nutritive value of a meal can be judged.

Knowledge of the basic elements (balance, unity, rhythm, etc.) which can be used to judge a work of art.

Knowledge of the criteria by which home economists judge the relative proportions of income distributed for different purposes by a family.

1.25 - Knowledge of Methodology

Knowledge of the methods of inquiry, techniques, and procedures employed in a particular subject field as well as those employed in investigating particular problems and phenomena. --Here, again, the emphasis is on the individual's knowledge of the methods rather than on his ability to use the methods in the ways defined by categories 3.00 to 6.00. However, the student is frequently required to know about methods and techniques and to know the ways in which they have been used. Such knowledge is most nearly of an historical or encyclopedic type. This knowledge, although simpler and perhaps less functional than the ability to actually employ the methods and techniques, is an important prelude to such use. Thus before engaging in an inquiry the student may be expected to know about the methods and techniques which have been employed in similar inquiries. At a later stage in his inquiry he may be expected to show relations between the methods he has employed and the methods employed by others.

1.25 <u>Knowledge of Methodology</u>--Illustrative Educational Objectives

The student shall know the methods of attack relevant to the kinds of problems of concern to the social sciences.

Knowledge of scientific methods for evaluating health concepts.

Knowledge of the techniques and methods used by scientists in seeking to answer questions about the world.

1.30 KNOWLEDGE OF THE UNIVERSALS
AND ABSTRACTIONS IN A FIELD

Knowledge of the major ideas, schemes, and patterns
by which phenomena and ideas are organized.--These are
the large structures, theories, and generalizations which
dominate a subject field or which are quite generally used
in studying phenomena or solving problems. These are at
the highest levels of abstraction and complexity.

These concepts bring together a large number of specific
facts and events, describe the processes and interrelations among these specifics, and thus enable the worker to
organize the whole in a parsimonious form.

These tend to be very broad ideas and plans which are
rather difficult for students to comprehend. Quite frequently
they are so difficult because the student is not thoroughly acquainted with the phenomena the universals are intended to
summarize and organize. If the student does get to know
them, however, he has a means of relating and organizing a
great deal of subject matter and as a result should have more
insight into the field as well as greater retentiveness for it.

1.31 - Knowledge of Principles and Generalizations

Knowledge of particular abstractions which summarize
observations of phenomena.--These are the abstractions
which are of greatest value in explaining, describing, predicting, or in determining the most appropriate and relevant
action or direction to be taken. Here all that is required is
that the student know the principle or generalization, that is,
that he be able to recognize or recall correct versions of
them. The actual application of these abstractions in problem
situations is included in 3.00 - Application. However, the recall of the principle or generalization as well as the recall of
the specific illustrations of them utilized in the instructional
material may be included in the present category.

1.31 Knowledge of Principles and Generalizations--Illustra-
tive Educational Objectives

Knowledge of the important principles by which our experience with biological phenomena is summarized.

The recall of major generalizations about particular cultures.

Knowledge of propositions, of fundamental logical principles, of propositional functions and quantifiers, and of sets.

Knowledge of the principles of chemistry which are relevant to life-processes and to health.

Knowledge of biological laws of reproduction and heredity.

Understanding of some of the principal elements in the heritage of Western civilization.

Knowledge of the major principles of high school chemistry.

To know the implications of our foreign trade policies for the international economy and for international goodwill.

To know the major principles involved in learning.

To become familiar with the plant illustrations of the principal laws of heredity and evolution.

To develop an understanding of such basic biological principles as cell theory, osmosis, and photosynthesis.

To develop a knowledge of the principles of federalism.

1.32 - Knowledge of Theories and Structures

Knowledge of the body of principles and generalizations together with their interrelations which present a clear, rounded, and systematic view of a complex phenomenon, problem, or field. --These are the most abstract formulations. They can be used to show the interrelation and organization of a great range of specifics. This category differs from 1.31 in that here the emphasis is on a body of principles and generalizations which are interrelated to form a theory or structure, while the principles and generalizations in 1.31 are treated as particulars which need not be related to each other.

1.32 Knowledge of Theories and Structures--Illustrative Educational Objectives

The recall of major theories about particular cultures.

Recall and recognition of what is contained in particular cultures.

Knowledge of the philosophic bases for particular judgments.

Understanding of the interrelations of chemical principles and theories.

To understand the structure and organization of Congress.

To understand the basic structural organization of the local city government.

Knowledge of a relatively complete formulation of the theory of evolution.

Testing for Knowledge, and illustrative test items

The major behavior tested in knowledge is whether or
not the student can remember and either cite or recognize
accurate statements in response to particular questions. Although somewhat more than rote memory is required for
knowledge, the form of the question and the level of precision
and exactness required should not be too different from the
way in which the knowledge was originally learned. This
means that the choices in the recognition form of question
must be at the level of discrimination originally intended by
the learning rather than at an entirely different level.

Probably the art of testing has been developed to the
greatest extent in the measurement of knowledge. This type
of behavior can be measured with great efficiency and economy, and a relatively small sample of problems and questions
in this area can be used to test a very large universe of knowledge. Some efforts have been made to explore the kinds of errors students make in their reactions to knowledge questions.
The analysis of such errors may frequently be useful in planning alternative choices for recognition questions, and the use
of scores or summaries of such errors may be useful in determining the accuracy and precision of the student's knowledge and the limits within which this knowledge may be said
to be known.

There is little point in making a very elaborate analysis
of the testing procedures which are appropriate here, since
most readers are quite familiar with adequate testing techniques for this purpose. For this reason, and for economy
of space, only a minimum number of test illustrations are offered with only occasional comments on specific features of
these illustrations.

1.00 - KNOWLEDGE -- ILLUSTRATIVE TEST ITEMS

1.10 Knowledge of Specifics

1.11 Knowledge of Terminology

1. A synapse can best be described as
    1. a mass or layer of protoplasm having many nuclei but lacking distinct cell boundaries.
    2. a lapse of memory caused by inadequate circulation of blood to the brain.
    3. the pairing of maternal with paternal chromosomes during maturation of the germ cells.
    4. the long cylindrical portion of an axon.
    5. the point at which the nervous impulse passes from one neuron to another.

2. Which one of the following phrases about wave motion defines period?
    1. The maximum distance a particle is displaced from its point of rest.
    2. The length of time required for a particle to make a complete vibration.
    3. The number of complete vibrations per second.
    4. The time rate of change of distance in a given direction.

Directions: In each group below, select the numbered word or phrase which most nearly corresponds in meaning to the word at the head of that group, and put its number in the parentheses at the right.

3. antelope
    1. fruit   2. animal   3. prelude   4. feeler   5. gallop
    . . . . . ( )

4. spaniel - type of
    1. sword   2. dog   3. lace   4. horse   5. coin
    . . . . . ( )

- - - -

1.12 Knowledge of Specific Facts

5. Jean Valjean was first sentenced to the galleys for stealing
    1. the Bishop's candlesticks.
    2. a loaf of bread.
    3. a few sticks of wood.
    4. a widow's cow.
    5. the cloth from off the altar.

6. The Monroe Doctrine was announced about ten years after the
    1. Revolutionary War.
    2. War of 1812.
    3. Civil War.
    4. Spanish-American War.

7. About what proportion of the population of the United States is living on farms?
    1. 10%   2. 20%   3. 35%   4. 50%   5. 60%

1.12 Knowledge of Specific Facts

Directions: The following paired statements refer to structures, functions, or factors which are to be compared in the quantitative sense.
Blacken answer space

    A- if the thing described on the left is greater than that on the right;

    B- if the thing described on the left is less than that on the right;

    C- if the left and the right are essentially the same.

8. Number of rabbits in   (A) is gr. than   number of foxes in the
   a food web   (B) is ls. than   same food web.
                 (C) is sa. as

9. Maximum size of food (A) is gr. than   maximum size of food
   particle that can be   (B) is ls. than   particle that can be eaten
   eaten by a sponge   (C) is sa. as   by a coelenterate.

10. Number of annual   (A) is gr. than   number of annual rings at
    rings at base of the   (B) is ls. than   point half-way up the trunk
    trunk of an old tree   (C) is sa. as   of the same tree.

- - - - -

11. A sodium ion differs from a sodium atom in that
    A- it is an isotope of sodium.
    B- it is more reactive.
    C- it has a positive charge on its nucleus.
    D- it exists only in solution.
    E- it has fewer electrons.

- - - - -

Directions: Blacken the answer space corresponding to the work of art which is earliest in date.

12. A- Browning's Fra Lippo Lippi
    B- Whitman's When Lilacs Last in the Dooryard Bloomed
    C- Tristan and Isolde
    D- Shelley's Ode to the West Wind
    E- Seurat's Sunday Afternoon on the Grande Jatte

- - - - -

Directions: For each of the following items, blacken answer space

    A- if it was in the Articles of Confederation;
    B- if it was in the Constitution of 1787;
    C- if it was in the Bill of Rights (Amendments I-X);
    D- if it was in Amendments XI-XXI;
    E- if it was in two or more of the above.

13. Protected life, liberty and property against governmental action without due process of law

14. Provided for popular election of United States Senators

15. Provided for a unicameral legislature

16. Gave the treaty-making power to Congress

1.20 Knowledge of Ways and Means of Dealing with Specifics

1.21 Knowledge of Conventions

Directions: Read each of the following groups of sentences carefully;
then decide which sentence in each group is better than the other sentences in that group.

17. 1. He was energetic and ambitious, his brother being lazy and indifferent.
    2. He was energetic and ambitious, but his brother was lazy and indifferent.
    3. He was energetic and ambitious, as his brother was lazy and indifferent.
    4. He was energetic and ambitious, and his brother was lazy and indifferent.

- - - - -

Directions: Select from the several choices given in each of the following items the one which you consider best.

18. I believe he (1) done, (2) did the best that he could.

- - - - -

19. Magnetic poles are usually named
    1. plus and minus.
    2. red and blue.
    3. east and west.
    4. north and south.
    5. anode and cathode.

20. For computation purposes, forces are frequently represented by
    1. straight lines.
    2. circles.
    3. arcs of a circle.
    4. angles.
    5. objects of three dimensions.

21. Which one of the following should not be classified as payment for the services of labor?
    1. The commissions earned by a real estate salesman
    2. The fee paid a justice of the peace for performing a marriage
    3. The dividend paid the owner of preferred stock
    4. The salary of a United States senator

Directions: Indicate whether each of the following statements is (1) a
fact (2) an opinion or judgment (3) neither a fact nor an opinion.

22. A man who works forty hours per week, fifty weeks per year, at one dollar per hour, earns an annual wage of $2000.

23. Many workers do not earn $2000 per year.

24. Unemployment insurance would provide some income for the families of unemployed workers.

25. The first movement of a sonata is commonly distinguished from the others by its greater
    1. rapidity and gayety.
    2. length and complexity.
    3. emotional abandon.
    4. sweetness and charm.
    5. structural informality.

Directions: Blacken one answer space for each item according to the following:
    A- if the statement applies to the symphonic poem;
    B- if the statement applies to the fugue;
    C- if the statement applies to the motet;
    D- if the statement applies to the suite;
    E- if the statement applies to the sonata.

26. Mozart's <u>Symphony in G Minor</u>, though composed for orchestra, is representative of this type in the number, order, and form of its various movements.

27. The minuet is the only dance movement commonly included in this musical type.

28. Instrumental works representative of this type are usually based upon extra-musical ideas, either poetic or descriptive.

29. A work of this type may include among its different movements an overture or prelude, an air, and a gigue.

— — — — — —

1.22 <u>Knowledge of Trends and Sequences</u>

30. During the process of breathing
    1. the air pressure outside is greater than that within the lungs at the end of an inhalation.
    2. the pressure within the lungs is greater than that outside at the end of an inhalation.
    3. the chest cavity has the smallest volume at the end of an inhalation.
    4. the air pressure within the lungs is greater than that outside at the end of an exhalation.
    5. the pressure inside and outside the lungs is equal at the end of an inhalation.

31. Which of the above curves represents the change of solubility of potassium nitrate with an increase in temperature? (Curves not shown here)
    1. AB
    2. CD
    3. EF
    4. GH
    5. IJ

32. The stages in the life history of the housefly are, in order,
   1. larva - egg - pupa - adult.
   2. pupa - larva - egg - adult.
   3. pupa - egg - larva - adult.
   4. egg - larva - adult - pupa.
   5. egg - larva - pupa - adult.

33. Which of the following best describes the policy of the government toward railroads in the twenty years following the Civil War?
   1. Purchase of railroads by the government after they had been privately financed and constructed
   2. Sale of publicly constructed railroads to private companies
   3. Granting of government subsidies to privately owned and constructed roads
   4. Little effort to encourage railroad construction

34. The latter part of the nineteenth century was notable for
   1. the consolidation of small businesses into larger organizations.
   2. the appearance of the "partnership" type of business organization.
   3. government restriction on unduly large profits.
   4. the decreased importance of the middleman between producer and consumer.

1.23 Knowledge of Classification and Categories

35. In all fairly complex animals the skeleton and the muscles are developed from the primary germ layer known as the
   1. ectoderm.   4. endoderm.
   2. neurocoele.   5. mesoderm.
   3. epithelium.

36. It is found that a specialized cell conducts impulses, but performs no other function well. Such a cell would best be classified as a(n)
   1. muscle cell.   4. cartilage cell.
   2. gland cell.   5. nerve cell.
   3. epithelial cell.

37. An engineer who designs houses is called
   1. a carpenter.   4. a draftsman.
   2. a civil engineer. 5. a mechanical engineer.
   3. an architect.

38. Which of the following is a chemical change?
   1. Evaporation of alcohol   4. Melting of wax
   2. Freezing of water   5. Mixing of sand and sugar
   3. Burning of oil

39. The branch of biological science which deals with the structure of living organisms is called
   1. physiology.   3. ecology.   5. embryology.
   2. pathology.   4. anatomy.

1.24 <u>Knowledge of Criteria</u> -- Illustrative Test Items

Directions: In the following, select the <u>one</u> <u>best</u> completion.

In the preface to the second edition of the <u>Critique</u> <u>of</u> <u>Pure</u> <u>Reason</u>, Kant discusses the problem of placing metaphysics upon the secure path of a science.

40. By science in this context he means
   A- a body of generalizations whose truth is guaranteed by ob-
      servation of facts.
   B- demonstrations of conclusions from assumptions which must
      always retain a hypothetical character.
   C- dialectic in the Platonic sense.
   D- a body of knowledge corresponding closely to the intellectual
      virtue called "scientific knowledge" by Aristotle.

41. In the view of John Ruskin, the greatest picture is
   A- that which imitates best.
   B- that which teaches us most.
   C- that which exhibits the greatest power.
   D- that which conveys the greatest number of the greatest ideas.

42. The criterion Darwin uses to distinguish the more variable species
   from the less variable species in Chapter II is
   A- number of individuals in the species.
   B- frequency of individual differences in the species.
   C- number of varieties in the species.
   D- number of closely related species.
   E- number of different climatic conditions tolerated by the
      species.

1.25 Knowledge of Methodology

43. A scientist discovers new facts by
   1. consulting the writings of Aristotle.
   2. thinking about the probabilities.
   3. making careful observations and conducting experiments.
   4. debating questions with his friends.
   5. referring to the works of Darwin.

44. We wish to know whether overeating affects the probable length of life. A scientific approach to this problem would be to
   1. see what the ancient Greek philosophers thought about the matter.
   2. perform a laboratory experiment with two groups of white rats, one group consistently overfed and the other group kept on a normal diet.
   3. ask fifty people selected at random and determine their average opinion.
   4. study food advertisements that relate to the problem.
   5. ask ten old people what they ate.

45. One use of the Periodic Table has been to
   1. determine the solubility of gases.
   2. find the degree of ionization of many compounds.
   3. predict undiscovered elements.
   4. determine molecular weights of compounds accurately.

46. When the scientist is confronted with a problem, his first step toward solving it should usually be to
   1. construct or purchase equipment.
   2. perform an experiment.
   3. draw conclusions.
   4. urge other scientists to cooperate with him in working it out.
   5. gather all available information on the subject.

47. Of the following, which represents the most important differences between the scientific method as used in the social sciences and as used in the natural sciences?
   1. Employment of the deductive rather than the inductive method of reasoning.
   2. Study of the developmental aspects of various problems.
   3. Necessity of regarding hypotheses as tentative in nature.
   4. Importance of understanding the problem of causation.
   5. Necessity of recognizing the value judgments of the investigator.

48. Stars are composed of the same elements as are found on the earth. Which of the following sources yields information supporting this statement?
   1. Observations of absorption spectra of dark interstellar matter.
   2. Observations of spectra of stars.
   3. Observations of brightness of stars.
   4. Observations of density of stars.
   5. Observations of the wave length of maximum radiation from stars.

49. Fossils in rocks constitute valuable clues to the past. Some of these fossils are identical with animals existing today. How does this affect the investigation of geological history?
     1. Such fossils make the work much simpler since they can be easily traced.
     2. These fossils are rare and therefore do not weaken the overall results very much.
     3. These fossils are extremely valuable since observation of their living counterparts yields much information as to climates and physical conditions of the geologic past.
     4. The existence of living counterparts of fossils is immaterial since only the fossil itself is important.

50. Which of the following provides the best method for determining the radius of a star?
     1. Measure the distance to the star and the diameter of the image of the star in a telescope of known length; the radius can be then obtained geometrically.
     2. Measure the distance, apparent brightness, and surface temperature. From the calculated brightness of a square centimeter of surface at that temperature and the absolute brightness, the area of the disk, and hence the radius is determined.
     3. The speed of rotation of the edge of disk of a rotating star can be measured from the Doppler shift. From this and the period of rotation the radius can be derived.
     4. In double stars the gravitational attraction depends on the density and the volume, hence the radius can be determined.

- - - - -

1.30 Knowledge of the Universals and Abstractions in a Field

1.31 Knowledge of Principles and Generalizations

51. Which of the following is the best description of the pattern of society in the 18th century colonies?
     1. A system of fixed castes ranging from the slave at the bottom through the indentured servant, the free workman, the small farmer, to the nobility at the top.
     2. A system of voluntary contracts among substantially equal individuals differentiated only by the amount of wealth they possessed.
     3. A hierarchy of social classes ranging from the nobility at the top, who controlled the society, to the indentured servant and slave at the bottom, who did the heavy work.
     4. A hierarchy of social classes in which individuals moved up and down with comparative ease and speed, except the black slaves, and in which a very large number objected to the continuance of well-defined classes.

52. Which <u>one</u> of the following is the best summary of Calhoun's views about the nature of the union?
    1. It is a compact formed between sovereign states, each of which retains the right to interpose its authority.
    2. It is a compact formed between sovereign states, but the states have no right to interpose.
    3. It is an instrument adopted by the American people, as one aggregate community.

53. If the volume of a given mass of gas is kept constant, the pressure may be diminished by
    1. reducing the temperature.
    2. raising the temperature.
    3. adding heat.
    4. decreasing the density.
    5. increasing the density.

54. Some generalizations concerning the common metals are that
    1. most of the metals form only one insoluble salt.
    2. all the simple salts of the alkali metals are soluble.
    3. the metals of the alkaline earth group are precipitated as carbonates.
    4. the alkali carbonates are insoluble in water.
    5. many of the heavy metal sulfides are insoluble in neutral or slightly acid solution.

55. Which of the following statements of the relationship between market price and normal price is true?
    1. Over a short period of time, market price varies directly with changes in normal price.
    2. Over a long period of time, market price tends to equal normal price.
    3. Market price is usually lower than normal price.
    4. Over a long period of time, market price determines normal price.

Directions: For items 56-59 select from the five principles at the right the most closely related principle and mark the corresponding answer space.

Statements	Principles
56. Fossils of primates first appear in the Cenozoic rock strata, while trilobite remains are found in the Protorozoic rocks.	1. There have been profound changes in the climate on the earth.
57. The Arctic and Antarctic regions are sparsely populated.	2. Coordination and integration of action is generally slower in plants than in animals.
58. Plants have no nervous system.	3. There is an increasing complexity of structure and function from lower to higher forms of life.
59. Large coal beds exist in Alaska.	4. All life comes from life and produces its own kind of living organisms.
	5. Light is a limiting factor to life.

1.32 <u>Knowledge of Theories and Structures</u>

Directions: Items 60-62 are concerned with possible evidences in support of the theory of biological evolution. Select from the key list the category to which the evidence mentioned in the item belongs.

      1. Comparative anatomy
      2. Comparative physiology
      3. Classification
      4. Embryology
      5. Paleontology

60. Intergrading forms of plants and animals differing from earlier species indicate that evolutionary change is probably taking place today in all living organisms.

61. Hematin crystals from the hemoglobin of various vertebrates have the same chemical composition.

62. The human heart has two chambers at a very early developmental stage.

2.00 - COMPREHENSION

Probably the largest general class of intellectual abilities and skills emphasized in schools and colleges are those which involve <u>comprehension</u>. That is, when students are confronted with a communication, they are expected to know what is being communicated and to be able to make some use of the material or ideas contained in it. The communication may be in oral or written form, in verbal or symbolic form, or, if we allow a relatively broad use of the term "communication," it may refer to material in concrete form as well as to material embodied on paper. For instance, we commonly expect comprehension of a physics demonstration, a geologic formation viewed on a field trip, a building illustrating a particular architectual feature, a musical work played by an orchestra. And, of course, we speak of comprehension of the above phenomena when presented in verbal, pictorial, or symbolic form on paper.

Although the term "comprehension" has been frequently associated with reading, e.g., reading comprehension, the use to which it is being put here is a somewhat broader one in that it is related to a greater variety of communications than that encompassed by written verbal materials. In another sense, the use of the term here is somewhat more limited than usual, since comprehension is not made synonymous with complete understanding or even with the fullest grasp of a message. Here we are using the term "comprehension" to include those <u>objectives</u>, <u>behaviors</u>, or <u>responses</u> which represent an understanding of the literal message contained in a communication. In reaching such understanding, the student may change the communication in his mind or in his overt responses to some parallel form more meaningful to him. There may also be responses which represent simple extensions beyond what is given in the communication itself.

Three types of comprehension behavior are considered here. The first is <u>translation</u> which means that an individual can put a communication into other language, into other terms, or into another form of communication. It will usually involve the giving of meaning to the various parts of a communication, taken in isolation, although such meanings may in part be determined by the context in which the ideas appear.

The second type of behavior is <u>interpretation</u> which involves dealing with a communication as a configuration of ideas whose comprehension may require a reordering of the ideas into a new configuration in the mind of the individual. This also includes thinking about the relative importance of the ideas, their interrelationships, and their relevance to generalizations implied or described in the original communication. Evidence of interpretation behavior may be found in the inferences, generalizations, or summarizations produced by the individual. Interpretation as here defined differs from analysis. In the latter the emphasis is on the form, the organization, the effectiveness, and the logic of the communication. It differs from application in that application is more definitely concerned with the meanings a communication has for other generalizations, situations, and phenomena, or the meanings that generalizations known by the student have for the communication. It differs from evaluation in that evaluation is characterized by the formulating of judgments explicitly based on criteria.

The third type of behavior to be considered under comprehension is <u>extrapolation.</u> It includes the making of estimates or predictions based on understanding of the trends, tendencies, or conditions described in the communication. It may also involve the making of inferences with respect to implications, consequences, corollaries and effects which are in accordance with the conditions described in the communication. It differs from application, however, in that the thinking is based on what is given rather than on some abstraction brought from the other experiences to the situation, such as a general principle or rule of procedure. Extrapolation may include judgments with respect to a universe where the communication characterizes a sample, or conversely with respect to a sample where the communication describes a universe. For the purpose of classification, interpolation may be regarded as a type of extrapolation in that judgments with respect to intervals within a sequence of data presented in a communication are similar to judgments going beyond the data in the usual sense of extrapolation.

Each of these types of educational objectives or behavior is further treated in the following.

2.10 Translation

Translation behavior occupies a transitional position between the behaviors classified under the category of knowledge and types of behavior described under the headings of
interpretation, extrapolation, analysis, synthesis, application, and evaluation. It will usually be found that individual
competence in translation is dependent on the possession of
the requisite or relevant knowledge. It is also true that unless an individual can give the denoted meaning to each of the
various parts of a communication and/or in terms of immediate or adjacent context, he will be unable to engage in more
complex thinking about the communication. For such thinking, a given term in a communication must symbolize for the
individual a general concept or even an aggregate of relevant
ideas. An abstract idea may need to be transformed to concrete or everyday terms to be useful in further thinking
about some problem presented by the communication. Sometimes an extended part of a communication may need to be
translated into briefer, or even more abstract, terms or
symbols, to facilitate thinking. This type of translation may
carry over into more complex behavior, such as analysis,
synthesis or application, when previous instruction has not
made such translation explicit. On the other hand, when
instruction has emphasized the particular points involved,
the translation may be more akin to simple recall of knowledge.

2.10 Translation -- Illustrative Educational Objectives

Translation from one level of abstraction to another

The ability to translate a problem given in technical or abstract phraseology into concrete or less abstract phraseology--"state the problem in your own words."

The ability to translate a lengthy part of a communication into briefer or more abstract terms.

The ability to translate an abstraction, such as some general principle, by giving an illustration or sample.

Translation from symbolic form to another form, or vice versa

The ability to translate relationships expressed in symbolic form, including illustrations, maps, tables, diagrams, graphs, and mathematical and other formulas, to verbal form and vice versa.

Given geometric concepts in verbal terms, the ability to translate into visual or spatial terms.

The ability to prepare graphical representations of physical phenomena or of observed or recorded data.

The ability to read musical scores.

The ability to read an architectural plan.

Translation from one verbal form to another

The ability to translate non-literal statements (metaphor, symbolism, irony, exaggeration) to ordinary English.

The ability to comprehend the significance of the particular words of a poem in the light of their context.

The ability to translate (with or without a dictionary) foreign language prose or poetry into good English.

2.20 Interpretation

In order to interpret a communication, the reader must first of all be able to translate each of the major parts of it--this includes not only the words and phrases, but also the various representational devices used. He must then be able to go beyond this part-for-part rendering of the communication to comprehend the relationships between its various parts, to reorder, or to rearrange it in his mind so as to secure some total view of what the communication contains and to relate it to his own fund of experiences and ideas. Interpretation also includes competence in recognizing the essentials and differentiating them from the less essential portions or from the relatively irrelevant aspects of the communication. This requires some facility in abstracting generalizations from a set of particulars as well as in weighing and assessing the relative emphasis to be given the different elements in the communication. In these respects, interpretation becomes synonymous with analysis and has characteristics in common with evaluation.

The essential behavior in interpretation is that when given a communication the student can identify and comprehend the major ideas which are included in it as well as understand their interrelationships. This requires a nice sense of judgment and caution to avoid reading into the document one's own ideas and interpretations. It also requires some ability to go beyond mere repetition and rephrasing of parts of the document to determine the larger and more general ideas contained in it. The interpreter must also recognize the limits within which interpretations can be drawn.

2.20 <u>Interpretation</u>--Illustrative educational objectives

The ability to grasp the thought of a work as a whole at any desired level of generality.

The ability to comprehend and interpret with increasing depth and clarity various types of reading material.

The ability to distinguish among warranted, unwarranted, or contradicted conclusions drawn from a body of data.

The ability to interpret various types of social data.

Ability in making proper qualifications when interpreting data.

2.30 Extrapolation

In preparing a communication, the writer attempts not only to state what he believes the truth of the matter to be, but also some of the consequences of it. While occasionally the writer is exhaustive, has detailed all of the conclusions to be drawn, and has indicated all of the possible consequences or implications of his ideas or material, this is rarely the case. Usually, the writer is unaware of or makes no effort to determine or state all of the conclusions to be drawn. The writer is limited in determining implications and consequences for new situations by his subject matter, which may be so general and widely applicable as to make impossible any attempt to explain all its ramifications, by his own lack of knowledge of all the possible situations in which it may be applied, and, finally, by the fact that he must in some ways limit his problem or presentations if he is to do an effective job.

The reader must, if he is to make full use of a communication, be able to extend it beyond the limits set by the writer as well as to apply some of the ideas of the communication to situations and problems not included explicitly in the communication. Mention was made earlier of extrapolation in the sense of thinking in terms of the relations between a sample and a universe and vice versa, and also of interpolation as akin to extrapolation where there are gaps in a sequence.

Accurate extrapolation requires that the reader be able to translate as well as interpret the document, and in addition, he must be able to extend the trends or tendencies beyond the given data and findings of the document to determine implications, consequences, corollaries, effects, etc., which are in accordance with the conditions as literally described in the original communication. Extrapolation requires that the reader be well aware of the limits within which the communication is posed as well as the possible limits within which it can be extended. In practically all cases, the reader must recognize that an extrapolation can only be an inference which has some degree of probability-- certainty with respect to extrapolations is rare.

Extrapolation as here defined is to be distinguished from application in that the thinking is characterized by the extension of that which is given to intermediate, past, future, or other conditions or situations. The thinking is usually less abstract than in the case of application where use is made of generalizations, rules of procedure, and the like.

2.30 <u>Extrapolation</u>--Illustrative educational objectives

The ability to deal with the conclusions of a work in terms of the immediate inferences made from the explicit statements.

The ability to draw conclusions and state them effectively. (Recognizing the limitations of the data, formulating accurate inferences and tenable hypotheses.)

Skill in predicting continuation of trends.

Skill in interpolation where there are gaps in data.

The ability to estimate or predict consequences of courses of action described in a communication.

The ability to be sensitive to factors which may render predictions inaccurate.

The ability to distinguish consequences which are only relatively probable from those for which there is a high degree of probability.

The ability to differentiate value judgments from predictions of consequences.

TESTING FOR COMPREHENSION, AND
ILLUSTRATIVE TEST ITEMS

Testing for translation objectives

In appraising student ability to translate technical terms, physics principles expressed in algebraic symbols, diagrams, or graphs by means of recall or recognition types of exercises, there may be clear-cut relationships between what is given and the response written or identified by the student. For example, terms may be listed and their definitions requested, or the definitions may be given and the student merely asked to recall or recognize the appropriate terms. In this situation the behaviors evaluated are equivalent to those listed under the category of knowledge, and this is particularly true where instruction has made explicit such formal associations. But these identical exercises may evaluate translation objectives which involve more than mere recall or recognition if instruction has been less formal and the thought processes of the student involve making new associations. For example, the answer to be selected as the definition of a term may be a definition which differs in phraseology from the formal one he has learned, and hence constitutes a novel situation.

Student ability to translate formal definitions or statements of principles may also be evaluated by exercises requiring him to recall or recognize correct illustrations or examples. But exercises requiring the selection of the "best" definition of a term may require more than the association of definition with term, if the student must judge the adequacy of the various definitions given. In still other types of exercises, more may be given than the terms or symbols and the student may have the advantage of contextual clues. Here again the nature of the previous instruction is the deciding factor rather than the appearance of the item. If the evaluation is to be of a behavior transcending knowledge, the context in which the terms or symbols appear must be to some extent novel context.

Additional complexity at the translation level of behavior occurs in certain types of exercises where more than one new term or symbol occurs and the student, while successively translating the terms or symbols, will need to consider their interrelationships. Item 18 on page 104 is an example of this sort of evaluation.

Evaluation of objectives at higher levels in the taxonomy is often impaired because of the student's inability to perform the initial step in problem solution: the translation of the problem into known terms. For example, the effectiveness of exercises used to evaluate application of general principles may be reduced because numerous students are unable to translate such terms as "Avogadro's principle," "Doppler effect," and "Gresham's law." For effective measurement where knowledge of such terms is not universal, the concepts they represent must be given in simpler or less abstract phraseology.

But even the simplest of demands given in either essay or objective exercises requires some translation for certain students. Experimentation has shown that some students are able to reduce or simplify the statement of the problem or to change it to language more characteristic of their own thinking without essentially changing the problem. But many students are unable to do such translation and may so distort the problem that they no longer are attempting to solve the same problem.[1] Evidence with respect to translation difficulties of the kinds described above may be obtained through use of appropriately worded essay exercises requiring the student to record the various steps in his thinking or it may be more effectively obtained through use of "thinking aloud" techniques for studying mental processes.

---

[1] Bloom, B. S., and Broder, Lois, Problem-solving processes of college students (A Supplementary Educational Monograph), Chicago: University of Chicago Press, Summer, 1950.

2.00 - COMPREHENSION -- ILLUSTRATIVE TEST ITEMS

2.10 <u>Translation from one level of abstraction to another.</u>

1. A group of examiners is engaged in the production of a taxonomy of educational objectives. In ordinary English, what are these persons doing?

    A- Evaluating the progress of education
    B- Classifying teaching goals
    C- Preparing a curriculum
    D- Constructing learning exercises

This exercise involves translation of "taxonomy" to "classification," a less abstract term. There is no context clue.

2. "The idea systems of primitive groups of people are highly restricted and traditional in content and, in addition, have been transmuted into customary ways of doing things." This best illustrates

    A- the stability of the primitive social organization.
    B- how primitive people evaluate the worth of ideas.
    C- the change of ideas to action.
    D- the repetition of customary ways of doing things.
    E- the slow progress of primitive peoples.

This requires translation of the term "transmuted" to the less abstract word "change" and here translation is aided by context clues.

3. When a current is induced by the relative motion of a conductor and a magnetic field, the direction of the induced current is such as to establish a magnetic field that opposes the motion. This principle is illustrated by

    A- a magnet attracting a nail.
    B- an electric generator or dynamo.
    C- the motion of a compass needle.
    D- an electric doorbell.

This involves translation of a formal and abstract definition by requiring the student to identify a concrete example.

4. While listening to lectures in physical science you have heard the following terms frequently used: "hypotheses," "theories," "scientific laws," "scientific method," and "scientific attitude." In a series of paragraphs, indicate in your own words and in terms of everyday experiences what these terms mean to you.

This exercise, an essay question, also involves the giving of concrete examples and also the behavior of "giving in your own words." Whether more than knowledge is required for the third and fourth exercises depends on previous instruction.

5. Which of the following represents the best definition of the term "protoplasm"?

   A- A complex colloidal system made up of water, proteins, and fats.
   B- Anything capable of growth by a regular progressive series of changes into a more complex unit.
   C- A complex mixture of proteins, fats, and carbohydrates, capable of responding to changes in its environment.
   D- A complex colloidal system of proteins, fats, carbohydrates, inorganic salts, and enzymes which manifests life.

This exercise requires judgment of the best definition of the term "protoplasm." The definitions given vary in correctness and completeness.

6. "All ideas are products of experience, or of reflection on experience. Sensations when given meaning are perceptions. Association of perceptions, or of simple ideas, leads to complex or abstract conceptions whose original source is still experience." This quotation best represents the point of view of

   A- positivism.
   B- rationalism.
   C- idealism.
   D- empiricism.
   E- pragmatism.

This requires the student to translate a concrete description of a type of philosophy to the abstract technical term standing for the type. This could involve mere recall, but may require more than recall if instruction has been characterized by no such brief summarization of the nature of empiricism.

7. When a beggar justifies his begging by the claim that the world owes him a living, he is

   A- behaving like a psychotic person.
   B- showing a paranoid symptom.
   C- having an hallucination.
   D- making a typical infantile reaction.
   E- rationalizing.

In this exercise a concrete example is given and the student required to identify the correct abstract term. More than knowledge is required if the example is new to the students.

2.10 Translation from symbolic form to another form, or vice versa

--after Darling

8. This cartoon best illustrates:

   A- Social problems are relative to time, place, and culture.
   B- The process of inventions is cumulative.
   C- Social problems are more prevalent in a dynamic society.
   D- There are differences in the rates of change between different phases of a culture.

9. The concept illustrated by the cartoon is

   A- technological progress.
   B- cultural lag.
   C- cultural diffusion.
   D- institutional maladjustment.

10. Newton's Law of Gravitation is expressed algebraically $F = G\dfrac{Mm}{d^2}$.

F represents force, M and m two masses, G is a constant, and d represents the distance between the masses. Assuming that M and m, as well as G, remain the same, or constant, which of the following graphs shows how the force changes as the distance between the masses varies?

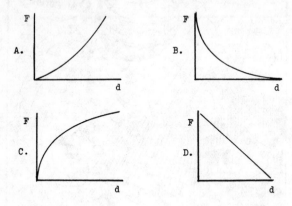

The exercise presented above illustrates translation from algebraic to geometric or graphic form. The exercises which follow involve translation from graphic to verbal form.

11. Which of the following graphs best represents the demand schedule of a typical commodity under competitive conditions?

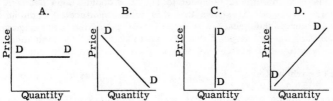

12. Which of the above graphs best represents the demand schedule of a commodity for which there is a perfectly inelastic demand?

13. Which of the following graphs best represents the supply schedule of a commodity under conditions of perfect competition?

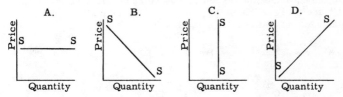

14. Which of the above graphs best represents the supply situation where a monopolist maintains a uniform price regardless of the amounts which people buy?

The following five formulas represent the structure of five different organic compounds. After the item number on the answer sheet, blacken the one lettered space which designates the compound to which each item correctly refers.

```
 H H H H          H H          H H H          H H H H          H   O
H-C-C-C-C-H     H-C-C-OH     H-C-C-C-H      H-C-C=C-C-H      H-C-C
 H H H H          H H          H | H           H   H          H   OH
                              H-C-H
                                H
```

    A.   B.   C.   D.   E.

15. The compound which can neutralize bases and forms salts.

16. The hydrocarbon which has the least tendency to "knock" among those listed above.

17. The compound which decolorizes bromine and potassium permanganate solution.

Note: While each of the formulas pertains to a specific organic compound, each of the compounds is representative of a type or class of compounds. The compound labeled B is but one of numerous alcohols. Hence each formula serves to symbolize a type. A student may say to himself with respect to D, "The double bond between two adjacent carbon atoms shows that this is an unsaturated compound. All such compounds react with bromine or potassium permanganate decolorizing them. Hence, the answer to 17 is D." Giving meaning to the double bond -C=C- is to translate the symbol for such a

union of carbon atoms. Similarly, $-C\overset{O}{\underset{OH}{\diagup}}$ signifies an organic acid

and leads to the conclusion that such a compound will neutralize a base and form a salt.

18. Coulomb's Law of Electrostatic Attraction states: "The force of attraction or repulsion between two charged bodies is directly proportional to the product of the charges, and inversely proportional to the square of the distance between them." If F is force, Q and Q' are charges, D is the dielectric constant and d is distance, a mathematical statement of the law is

A- $F = \dfrac{Q}{Dd^2}$ B- $F = \dfrac{QQ'}{D^2d}$ C- $F = \dfrac{QQ'}{Dd^2}$

D- $D = \dfrac{Q^2}{Fd}$ E- $d = \dfrac{QQ'}{DF}$

Note: If the student has memorized the equation given as answer C, mere recall is sufficient in selecting the correct answer. The correct answer can be obtained, however, through translation of the verbal statement to mathematical symbols.

2.10 Translation from one verbal form into another verbal form

19. "Milton! thou shouldst be living at this hour: England hath need of thee; she is a fen of stagnant waters" --Wordsworth.

The metaphor, "she is a fen of stagnant waters," indicates that Wordsworth felt that England was
A- largely swampy land.
B- in a state of turmoil and unrest.
C- making no progress.
D- in a generally corrupt condition.

-----

1   When I consider everything that grows
2   Holds in perfection but a little moment,
3   That this huge stage presenteth nought but shows
4   Whereon the stars in secret influence comment;
5   When I perceive that men as plants increase,
6   Cheered and checked even by the self-same sky;
7   Vaunt in their youthful sap, at height decrease,
8   And wear their brave state out of memory;
9   Then the conceit of this inconstant stay
10 Sets you most rich in youth before my sight,
11 Where wasteful Time debateth with Decay,
12 To change your day of youth to sullied night;
        And all in war with Time for love of you,
        As he takes from you, I engraft you new.
            (Shakespeare, Sonnet XV)

20. In the first two lines Shakespeare says that

    A- all living things are examples of the perfection of nature.
    B- every living thing retains perfection only for a very brief time.
    C- man, part of all living things, is basically not perfect.
    D- all living things show the characteristics of evolution.

21. In lines 3 and 4, the poet says that

    A- life, which is subject to the laws of nature, is ephemeral and transitory, like a play.
    B- all the world's a stage, whose lighting is given by the stars.
    C- man, a character in a great drama, is controlled by the "stars," that is, destiny.
    D- the stage of the universe is controlled by the laws of nature.

Note: The original series included three more exercises relevant to other lines in the sonnet. Here the student is expected to make use of the context in order to determine the appropriate translation.

------

22. Das Gut gehört immer noch dem Grossvater:

    A- Grandfather still hears well.
    B- Grandfather always hears good things.
    C- The estate still belongs to grandfather.
    D- The good people always listen to grandfather.
    E- The goods still belong to grandfather.

Note: The student is expected to select the English sentence which represents the best translation of the German sentence. Similar exercises may be written with an English sentence as the item stem and German sentences as the answers. The same type of exercise could be extended to the use of brief paragraphs as item stems and as answers. In every case, as is true of answer C of exercise 22, the best answer should be more than a literal translation.

Testing for interpretation objectives, and illustrative test items

In evaluating the ability to interpret, the individual is presented with a communication and is asked to supply or recognize inferences which may be drawn from the communication. The inferences may be at a more general level than the communication itself and should, where possible, be based on more than one element in the communication. Sometimes, the inferences may represent generalizations based on particulars given in the communication, or may pertain to particulars to which generalizations given in the communication apply.

Essay exercises can be used in the evaluation of student ability to interpret. The essay exercise should accompany the communication to be interpreted and this communication may be one or more quoted paragraphs, a cartoon, a graph, or a table of numerical data. For example, a student may be asked to compare or contrast the points of view of Hamilton and Jefferson with respect to the powers of the National Government given quotations from The Federalist and from the Second Inaugural. The interpretation of a lengthy quotation may be that of preparing a summary or outline. One or more cartoons may be the basis for an essay exercise requiring the student to interpret the cartoons with respect to some contemporary social problem or issue. Similarly, graphs or tables with appropriately worded essay questions may require the student to interpret the data thus presented and to draw inferences from them respecting their interrelationship or meaning as a whole.

Objective exercises can also be used in the evaluation of interpretation ability. Thus, the exercises which follow the quoted paragraphs, cartoons, tables, or graphs may either be any of the more usual objective types, for example, the multiple choice, or students may be asked to classify items relevant to the quoted material according to certain categories. As an example of the latter, if two selections are given, the student may be asked to classify items as "true of the first selection," "true of the second selection," "true of both selections," and "true of neither selection." The items

may be inferences which correctly pertain to interrelationships in either or both of the selections or they may be incorrect inferences or generalizations. A second example
employs a very useful type of direction, particularly where
the quoted material in paragraph form presents scientific
data, or such data are presented in tabular or graphic form.
It requests the student to classify items according to whether
or not the data are sufficient to prove the truth or falsity of
the items or are insufficient for such judgments. Frequently,
the categories ask the students to judge each item with
respect to whether the given data definitely support its truth,
indicate that the item is probably true, definitely reveal that
it is false, indicate that it is probably false, or whether the
data are insufficient for any judgment with respect to the
truth or falsity of the item. These categories may be ordered
in the form of a scale: (1) definitely true, (2) probably
true, (3) insufficient evidence, (4) probably false, (5) definitely false. [2]

Test scores differentiating between "crude errors," "go-
ng beyond the data," and "over-caution" are especially use-
ul in evaluating student skill in interpretation since such
scores may be relatively independent of knowledge of content
and may be valid measures of modes of operation and generalized techniques for dealing with materials and problems.
If the categories are in the order suggested at the close of
he preceding paragraph, "going beyond the data," or the
endency to over-generalize may be evaluated by counting
incorrect answers which are in the direction of the extremes
of the scale. Over-caution is evaluated by counting incorrect
answers which are in the direction of the center of the scale.
The tendency to make "crude errors" is evaluated by counting incorrect answers which traverse the center of the scale.

---

[2] Use of this type of item, however, should be limited
to instances in which the student is given some pre-test
training in the proper use of these terms. Otherwise, the
tendency to use "probably true" or "probably false" to express the student's doubt about his own answer, as opposed
to doubt about the data's completeness, tends to obscure
proper interpretation of the results.

(See the notes which follow the first of the illustrative series of the exercises of this type.) Exercises of the type just described usually ask the student to make his judgments or interpretations only on the basis of the data given. Occasionally, the student is asked to evaluate the truth or falsity of items in terms of both the given data and in terms of whatever other knowledge he possesses. Items 49-58 of the illustrative exercises given on the following pages permit the use of other knowledge in the interpretation of the data given.

Consumers' Price Index, 1918-49
(1935 - 39 = 100)

Per Cent   Per Cent

Source: U.S. Dept. of Labor,
Bureau of Labor Statistics

Making your judgments only in terms of the information given in the graph, classify each of the following items by blackening space

    A- if the item is <u>definitely</u> true;
    B- if the item is <u>probably</u> true;
    C- if the information given is not sufficient to indicate any
        degree of truth or falsity in the item;
    D- if the item is <u>probably false</u>;
    E- if the item is <u>definitely false</u>.

23. People were better off in 1932 than in 1949.
24. Since 1918 to the present, the dollar was most valuable in 1933.
25. More prices went up than went down between 1932 and 1940.
26. Men in the age group of 30-40 made the most income gains in the past decade.
27. In 1940-46 some loss in real income was most probably incurred by people living on interest from bonds.
28. More prices went down than went up between 1926 and 1929.
29. Anyone living on a fixed income was much worse off in 1949 than in 1940.

<u>Note</u>: "Going beyond the data" requires a count of B items marked A, C items marked A, B, D, or E, and D items marked E. "Overcaution" requires a count of A items marked B, B and D items marked C, and E items marked D. Evaluation of "crude errors" requires a count of A and B items marked D or E and D or E items marked A or B.

DIRECTIONS: Below are some statistics relating to education and occupations. You are to judge what conclusions may be drawn from them.

OCCUPATIONS	Occupational distribution found in a sample of male college graduates*	Distribution of occupations in the population as a whole, 1950
	PERCENTAGES	
Executives, minor officials, partners, proprietors	23.5	9.1
Professional workers	51.3	4.7
Salesmen	6.0	Less than 1%
Skilled workers	7.1	33.8
Clerical workers	8.7	13.4
Unskilled workers	1.7	26.1
Farmers	1.7	13.0
	100.0	100.0

*You may assume that the sample selected is representative of all male college graduates in the United States.

Below are a series of statements relating to occupations and education. Blacken answer space

    A- if the foregoing statistics alone are sufficient to prove the statement true;
    B- if the foregoing statistics alone are sufficient to indicate that the statement is probably true;
    C- if the foregoing statistics alone are not sufficient to indicate whether there is any degree of truth or falsity in the statement;
    D- if the foregoing statistics alone are sufficient to indicate that the statement is probably false;
    E- if the foregoing statistics alone are sufficient to prove the statement false.

30. Typically farmers are completely uneducated.

31. The professions absorb a larger percentage of male college graduates than any other group in the country.

32. Sons of unskilled workers and sons of farmers have an approximately equal chance to go to college.

33. Educational opportunity for the lower classes is increasing.

34. The same proportions of farmers and of unskilled workers are college graduates.

DIRECTIONS: The following generalizations are sometimes inferred from the foregoing statistics on occupations and education. You are to judge whether or not the generalizations made below can be made on the basis of these data alone or if certain additional data are needed. For the following items, <u>blacken</u> answer space

A- if the generalization can be made on the basis of the foregoing statistics, without any additional information.

B- if in addition to or instead of the foregoing statistics you would need to know the percentage of people in each occupation who were unable to attend college.

C- if in addition to or instead of the foregoing statistics you would need to know the percentage of male college graduates in each occupation whose fathers were college graduates **and were in** the same occupation.

D- if the generalization <u>cannot</u> properly be made even if the additional information described in B and C were available.

35. Unskilled, skilled and clerical workers do not value college education as much as do businessmen.

36. The low percentage of college graduates in the skilled, clerical, and unskilled worker class reveals a lack of social mobility in America.

37. Higher education provides a medium in this country whereby some youth improve their status.

38. Children of business and professional men have a greater opportunity to enter well-paid occupations.

39. Social mobility in the United States is increasing.

- - - - - - -

A scientist cultivated a large colony of disease-producing bacteria. From them, he extracted a bacteria-free material referred to as substance X. A <u>large</u> dose of substance X was then injected into each of a group of animals (group A). These animals promptly developed some of the symptoms normally produced in infection by the bacteria in question. Then, into each of a number of other animals (group B), the scientist made a series of injections of <u>small</u> doses of substance X. Three weeks after this series of injections, and continuing for two years thereafter, this group of animals (group B) could be made to develop the disease by injecting them with several thousand times the number of bacteria which was fatal to untreated animals.

After the item number on the answer sheet, blacken space

A- if the data given above definitely show that the item correctly completes the introductory statement.

B- if the data given above do not definitely show that the item correctly completes the introductory statement.

(Be careful to make your judgments in terms of the data given in the description of the experiment.)

Substance X acted upon the animals of group A as if it were a

40. poison.
41. destroyer of poisons.
42. stimulator causing animals of group A to produce destroyers of the bacterial poison.

With reference to its effect upon the animals of group B, substance X appeared to act as

43. a means of counteracting the effects of the disease-producing bacteria.
44. if it were a destroyer of the bacteria or of their poisonous products.
45. if it were a poisonous product of the bacteria.

Ten months after the series of injections described above, the scientist prepared serum from the blood of the animals of group B. He injected this serum into each of a large group (group C) of animals infected with the disease. A control group, also infected with the disease, was given no serum. There was a higher percentage of prompt recoveries in group C than in the control group.

Serum from the animals of group B acted in the animals of group C to

46. stimulate the animals of group C to produce a destroyer of the disease-producing bacteria or their poisonous products.
47. destroy the disease-producing bacteria or their poisonous products.
48. hasten the deleterious effects of the disease-producing bacteria upon animals of group C.

"Supply and demand are determined in large part by the marginal consumers and marginal producers. If a tax is levied only on nonmarginal producers it does not materially increase the costs of production of the marginal producers, and does not, therefore, greatly influence the price to the public. In other words, the tax in such a case cannot readily be shifted. A tax on net income is such a tax. Those who have no net income are not taxed and their costs of production are not increased. They continue to produce at no increase in costs. It is their costs that determine primarily the price of the product. Those who pay the tax on net income, being nonmarginal producers, find it impossible or exceedingly difficult to pass the tax on to the consumers in the form of higher prices.

"A sales tax, on the other hand, does raise the costs of production of the marginal producers, causing them to withdraw from production unless the tax can be shifted in the form of higher prices to the consumer. If some withdraw from production, the supply will decrease and the price will increase sufficiently to absorb the sales tax."

--Quoted from Introduction to Social Science
by Atteberry, Auble, Hunt, and others.

After the item number on the answer sheet, blacken space

A- if the item is true and its truth is supported by information given in the paragraph.

B- if the item is true, but its truth is not supported by information given in the paragraph.

C- if the item is false and its falsity is supported by information given in the paragraph.

D- if the item is false, but its falsity is not supported by information given in the paragraph.

49. Marginal producers are less affected by a sales tax than by an income tax.

50. Nonmarginal producers find it difficult to pass a tax on net income on to the consumer in the form of higher prices, because consumers will then buy largely from marginal producers.

51. An income tax has less effect on prices than a sales tax.

52. Taxes on luxuries can be more readily shifted to the consumer than taxes on necessities.

53. The two paragraphs assume conditions of free competition.

54. Marginal producers pay no tax on net income.

55. Nonmarginal producers can pass a sales tax to consumers in the form of higher prices, because the marginal producers must also raise prices or withdraw from competition.

56. A decrease in price has the same effect on marginal consumers that it has on marginal producers.

An anthropologist wishes to discover whether there are intelligence differences between white people and Negroes. He administers a standard group intelligence test to all of the students in alternate grades of a small town school system which includes a public junior college. His results are presented in the following table:

Grade	White students No. taking test	White students Ave. I. Q.	Negro students No. taking test	Negro students Ave. I. Q.
1	300	103	75	85
3	275	99	60	90
5	260	101	35	105
7	240	108	20	115
H. S. Soph.	215	115	10	125
H. S. Senior	200	120	8	135
J. C. 2nd yr.	100	125	3	145

On the basis of the data in this table, the anthropologist formulates a number of conclusions. Some of these are given below, together with possible comments which might have been made by consulting scientists called in to evaluate his work. For each of these numbered conclusions, blacken the answer space corresponding to the one comment which might appropriately be made in such an evaluation.

57. Some Negroes are more intelligent than most people.

   A- This conclusion is valid.
   B- This is probably true, but one cannot be sure, because the Negroes included in the study are a selected group.
   C- This is probably true, but one cannot be sure, because both Negroes and whites included in the study are a selected group.
   D- This is probably untrue, since the average I.Q. for 1st grade Negroes is 18 points lower than for 1st grade whites.
   E- The comparison is valid only if there are no real qualitative differences between the white and Negro mind.

58. Before beginning schooling, Negro children in this community are less intelligent than white children.

   A- This conclusion is valid.
   B- This conclusion is valid, provided the children who enter first grade are typical of the children of each race.
   C- This conclusion is valid provided the children who enter first grade are typical of the children of each race, and provided the items on the test do not really measure skills which white children have a better chance to learn.
   D- This conclusion is valid, provided the children who enter first grade are typical of the children of each race, and provided some Negroes were included in the group originally used in standardizing the test.

Note: The original series included seven more exercises relevant to the data given above.

59.

The first paragraph below is quoted from an inaugural address by Thomas Jefferson; the second paragraph is taken from one of the essays in The Federalist, written by Alexander Hamilton. Read these quotations for the purpose of identifying the major controversial issue inherent in them. Then write a brief essay in which you indicate the current importance and implications of this issue.

I

"About to enter, fellow-citizens, on the exercise of duties which comprehend everything dear and valuable to you, it is proper you should understand what I deem the essential principles of our Government, and consequently those which ought to shape its Administration. I will compress them within the narrowest compass they will bear, stating the general principle, but not all its limitations. Equal and exact justice to all men, of whatever state or persuasion, religious or political; peace, commerce, and honest friendship with all nations, entangling alliances with none; the support of the State governments in all their rights, as the most competent administrations for our domestic concerns and the surest bulwarks against anti-republican tendencies; the preservation of the General Government in its whole constitutional vigor, as the sheet anchor of our peace at home and safety abroad; a jealous care of the right of election by the people--a mild and safe corrective of abuses which are lopped by the sword of revolution where peaceable remedies are unprovided; absolute acquiescence in the decisions of the majority, the vital principle of republics, from which is no appeal but to force, the vital principle and immediate parent of despotism; a well-disciplined militia, our best reliance in peace and for the first moments of war, till regulars may relieve them; the supremacy of the civil over the military authority; economy in the public expense, that labor may be lightly burthened; the honest payment of our debts and sacred preservation of the public faith; encouragement of agriculture, and of commerce as its handmaid; the diffusion of information and arraignment of all abuses at the bar of the public reason; freedom of the press; the freedom of person under the protection of the habeas corpus, and trial by juries impartially selected. These principles form the bright constellation which has gone before us and guided our steps through an age of revolution and reformation."

II

"The result of these observations to an intelligent mind must be clearly this, that if it be possible at any rate to construct a federal government capable of regulating the common concerns, and preserving the general tranquillity, it must be founded, as to the objects committed to its care, upon the reverse of the principle contended for by the opponents of the proposed constitution. It must carry its agency to the persons of the citizens. It must stand in need of no intermediate legislations; but must itself be empowered to employ the arm of the ordinary magistrate to execute its own resolutions. The majesty of the national authority must be manifested through the medium of the courts of justice. The government of the union, like that of each state, must be able to address itself immediately to the hopes and fears of individuals; and to attract to its support those passions which have the strongest influence upon the human heart. It must, in short, possess all the means, and have a right to resort to all the methods, of executing the powers with which it is entrusted, that are possessed and exercised by the governments of the particular states."

60.   -----

The following selection from the writings of Descartes contains his explanations of certain phenomena. State which of his explanations are still accepted as valid, and indicate which of his explanations are no longer accepted, pointing out briefly how they have been modified.

"Those who have acquired even the minimum of medical knowledge know how the heart is composed, and how all the blood in the veins can easily flow from the vena cava into its right side and from thence into the lung by the vessel we term the arterial vein, and then return from the lung into the left side of the heart, by the vessel called the venous artery, and finally pass from there into the great artery, whose branches spread throughout all the body .... We know that all movements of the muscles, as also all the senses, depend on the nerves, which resemble small filaments, or little tubes, which all proceed from the brain, and thus contain like it a certain very subtle air or wind which is called the animal spirits.... So long as we live there is a continual heat in our heart, which is a species of fire which the blood of the veins there maintains, and this fire is the corporeal principle of all the movements of our members.... Its first effect is to dilate (expand) the blood with which the cavities of the heart are filled; that causes this blood, which requires a greater space for its occupation, to pass into the great artery; then when this dilation (expansion) ceases, new blood immediately enters from the vena cava into the right cavity of the heart, and from the venous artery into the left cavity.... The new blood which has entered into the heart is then immediately afterward rarefied (expanded) in the same manner as that which preceded it; and it is just this which causes the pulse, or beating of the heart and arteries; so that this beating repeats itself as often as the new blood enters the heart. It is also just this which gives its motion to the blood, and causes it to flow ceaselessly and very quickly in all the arteries and veins, whereby it carries the heat which it acquires in the heart to all parts of the body, and supplies them with nourishment."

61.   -----

The cartoon strip reproduced below portrays an episode in the life of Andy Gump. Write a paragraph in which you tell how you as a physiologist would explain Andy's reaction to the presence of the bear.

THE GUMPS—BEARING UP

Testing for extrapolation objectives, and illustrative test items

It is often effective to test for extrapolation while testing ability to interpret through use of essay or objective exercises of the type earlier described and illustrated. The exercises on extrapolation then attempt to determine whether or not the student can go beyond the limits of the data or information given and make correct applications and extensions of the data or information. It is to be expected that the extrapolations will differ from the original in some of the following respects:

A. Time dimension--if the data given contain trends and tendencies within a given time range, the extrapolation will represent an attempt to extend the trends and tendencies to other time periods (including time periods within a sequence).

B. Topic or domain--if the communication deals with one topic or subject, the extrapolation may represent an attempt to extend the ideas to another topic or situation which is relevant. This is more than altering the form of the communication, since it involves extending the ideas beyond the original topic or subject.

C. Sample or universe--if the data deal with a sample, the extrapolation may pertain to the universe from which the sample is drawn. Conversely, if the data pertain to a universe, the extrapolation may pertain to a sample. For example, data may be given with respect to the trends in production of automobiles over a period of years, while the extrapolation may pertain to the production of Ford cars.

2.30 Extrapolation

In the chart given below, amounts spent for any given state function all read from the base line. For example, interest and retirement of the state debt required the expenditure of 40 million dollars in 1938, rather than 40 million minus 21.

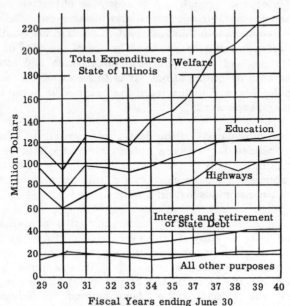

Fiscal Years ending June 30

After the number on the answer sheet corresponding to that of each statement, blacken space

    A if the information given in the chart is sufficient for a judgment that the statement is definitely true.

    B if the information given in the chart is sufficient only to indicate that the statement is probably true.

    C if the information given in the chart is not sufficient to indicate any degree of truth or falsity in the statement.

    D if the information given in the chart is sufficient for a judgment that the statement is probably false.

    E if the information given in the chart is sufficient for a judgment that the statement is definitely false.

62. Less money was spent in 1930 than before 1929 for welfare and education.

63. In 1931 and 1932 the expenditure of money for highway purposes was evidently considered a means of combatting the depression.

64. Had our country not entered the war in 1941, expenditures for welfare in 1942 would have been greater than in 1940.

65. In 1940 a much greater proportion of the total expenditures were for welfare than in 1942.

66. The increasing amount of money spent by the State for all purposes between 1929 and 1940 must have come from sources other than borrowing.

67. Less money was spent by the State in 1930 than in 1929 almost wholly because of retrenchment with respect to highway expenditures.

68. Less money was spent for highways in 1931 than in 1932.

69. Unemployment increased in the State between 1937 and 1939.

70. Increase in expenditures from 1929 to 1940 has been the least in those classified under interest and retirement of State debt.

71. The per capita expenditures of Illinois cities for welfare and for education parallel the State expenditures for these two purposes.

72. The total expenditures of the State in 1940 exceeded one-half billion dollars.

73. The State debt increased little between 1933 and 1940 as compared to expenditures for education.

This is an example in which translation, interpretation, and extrapolation are all included. Items 62, 64, 65, 69, and 71 are examples of extrapolation. Item 71 is an example of extrapolating from universe to sample.

- - - - - -

74. Contrast the kinds of interpretation one can make from frequency polygons or histograms and smoothed curves drawn from the same distribution of test scores obtained from a sample of eighth grade pupils.

75. The ratios of employed persons to unemployed are given for each year over an interval of several years. Why is such data inadequate in revealing the employment status of auto-workers, lumbermen, harvest hands, and calendar salesmen?

76. Immigrants tend to settle in the slum areas closest to the central business districts of our large cities. Where are their descendants most likely to be found?

- - - - - -

3.00 APPLICATION

The whole cognitive domain of the taxonomy is arranged in a hierarchy, that is, each classification within it demands the skills and abilities which are lower in the classification order. The application category follows this rule in that to apply something requires "Comprehension" of the method, theory, principle, or abstraction applied. Teachers frequently say, "If a student really comprehends something, then he can apply it." To make the distinction between the "Comprehension" and "Application" categories clear, we have described it in two ways.

One way of looking at the distinction is this. A problem in the comprehension category requires the student to know an abstraction well enough that he can correctly demonstrate its use when specifically asked to do so. "Application," however, requires a step beyond this. Given a problem new to the student, he will apply the appropriate abstraction without having to be prompted as to which abstraction is correct or without having to be shown how to use it in that situation. A demonstration of "Comprehension" shows that the student <u>can</u> use the abstraction when its use is specified. A demonstration of "Application" shows that he <u>will</u> use it correctly, given an appropriate situation in which no mode of solution is specified.

A second way of looking at this is demonstrated in Figure I. It shows in diagrammatic form the problem-solving process of answering questions classified in the "Application" category. In the complete solution of an "Application" problem, all 6 steps are involved. Whether the process more closely resembles the left or right side of the chain at steps 1 and 2 would depend upon the student's familiarity with the problem. Steps 1 through 4 are part of "Application" but not of "Comprehension." Comprehension is best represented by a problem which starts with step 5, steps 1-4 being unnecessary because of the structuring of the problem situation.

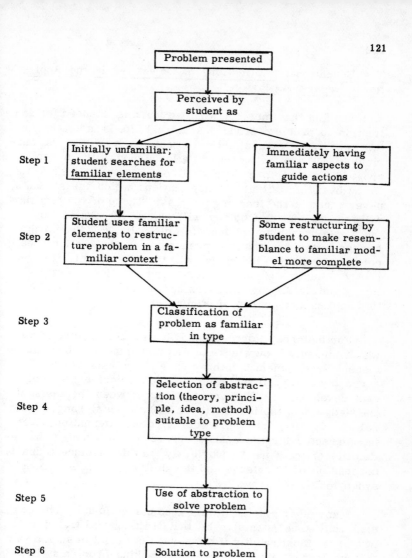

Figure I

The Educational Implications of Objectives in the Application Category

The fact that most of what we learn is intended for application to problem situations in real life is indicative of the importance of application objectives in the general curriculum. The effectiveness of a large part of the school program is therefore dependent upon how well the students carry over into situations applications which the students never faced in the learning process. Those of you familiar with educational psychology will quickly recognize this as the age-old problem of transfer of training. Research studies have shown that comprehending an abstraction does not certify that the individual will be able to apply it correctly. Students apparently also need practice in restructuring and classifying situations so that the correct abstraction applies (steps 1-4 of Figure I).

For instance, Horrocks and Troyer constructed a test which measured knowledge of fact and principle about adolescent development and three case study tests which measured the ability to apply the facts and principles of adolescent development. The correlations between the tests of knowledge and application (over 100 students) ranged from .31 to .54 after they were corrected for attenuation, that is, corrected for the chance errors which affected the reliability of tests used. Obviously, in this instance at least, possession of knowledge and the ability to apply it are not synonymous. [1]

Many other studies in this area can be found. The general consensus seems to be that training will transfer to new areas most readily if the person is taught in such a way that he learns good methods of attacking problems, if he learns concepts and generalizations (rather than how to use certain facts in specific instances), if he learns proper attitudes toward work, and if he develops proper attitudes of self-confidence and control. It is obvious that the objectives in

---

[1] John E. Horrocks, "The Relationship between Knowledge of Human Development and the Use of Such Knowledge," Journal of Applied Psychology, 30, (1946), 501-507.

the application category, as they embody the meaning of transfer of training, are extremely important aspects of the curriculum. Further, the evaluation of the extent to which the application outcomes are being achieved becomes one of the most important aspects of the entire evaluation process. For, to the extent that the evaluation process gives the schools information concerning success or failure in this aspect of the curriculum, evaluation provides a feedback for future curricular revision. Such feedback is of the utmost importance as a basis for appropriate revision of the educational process.

3.00 <u>Application</u> -- Illustrative Educational Objectives

Looking over collections of teachers' objectives leads to the generalization that objectives in the application area sound very much alike, regardless of the subject matter involved. For this reason only a few examples are given below. No examples are given from the humanities field since the only examples that could be found used application of a principle as only a part (often minor) of a process, e.g., as in creating a piece of artwork (synthesis) or judging a piece of artwork (evaluation).

Application to the phenomena discussed by a paper, of the scientific terms and concepts used in other papers.

The ability to apply social science generalizations and conclusions to actual social problems.

The ability to predict the probable effect of a change in a factor on a biological situation previously at equilibrium.

The ability to apply science principles, postulates, theorems, or other abstractions to new situations.

Employing experimental procedures in finding the solutions to problems and the answers to questions in making home repairs.

Apply principles of psychology in identifying the characteristics of a new social situation.

The ability to relate principles of civil liberties and civil rights to current events.

Skill in applying principles of democratic group action to participation in group and social situations.

The ability to apply the laws of trigonometry to practical situations.

To develop some skill in applying Mendel's laws of inheritance to experimental findings on plant genetic roblems.

Testing for Application, and illustrative test items

Experience in testing for application behavior has shown that several factors must be routinely taken into consideration. Some of them are as follows:

Need for new yet real items

If the situations described by the objective or by the testing situation are to involve application as we are defining it here, then they must either be situations new to the student or situations containing new elements as compared to the situation in which the abstraction was learned. If the situations presented the student to test "application" are old ones in which he originally learned the meaning of the abstraction, the student does not have to "apply" the abstraction. Rather, he needs merely to recall the original situation in which he learned the abstraction, a behavior herein classified as knowledge or a level in comprehension. This is likely to mean that the problem must either (a) be posed in a situation which is fictional, (b) be one which is drawn from material with which the student is not likely to have yet had contact, or (c) be on a problem known to the student but a new slant that he is unlikely to have thought of previously. Ideally we are seeking a problem which will test the extent to which the individual has learned to apply the abstraction in a practical way. This means that the problems should have some relation to the situations in which he may ultimately be expected to apply the abstractions. The kinds of problems that come from the three above sources do not always meet this criterion. To the extent that fictional problem situations--(a) above--are unreal, contrary to fact, or bizarre they do not seem as likely to elicit valid behavior as situations of a more common and realistic nature. Situations drawn from material with which the student is not yet likely to have had contact--(b) above-- are usually drawn from advanced material and simplified for use in an earlier grade. It is frequently difficult to sufficiently simplify the situations and yet retain their reality. Further, the bright student often blocks this source of new situations by having read ahead or done outside reading, and so familiarized himself and sometimes his playmates with them. The new slant on common situations--(c) above-- probably represents our most suitable source of new, yet realistic items. They are, however, extremely hard to devise. The PEA Application of Principles Test used this source of items.

General problem-solving ability vs. application of specific principles

If one is teaching a particular body of principles and wishes to evaluate the effect of this instruction, one is interested not so much in the extent to which the student solves the problem by common sense or the use of commonly known information, but rather in the extent to which the student has directly benefited from the specific learning situations used. Problems which within themselves contain clues as to how they should be solved (such clues being interpretable by someone with little or no specialized knowledge) would not test application of the principles one has taught. One can determine the extent to which the test is not evaluating as desired by administering the items to persons who have not undergone the instruction in the area taught but who, nevertheless, are persons equal in general ability to those for whom the application items are designed.

Diagnosing failure on application problems

As is true of any test result, the indication that a student is unable to solve application problems may result from a number of causes besides the one that the student has failed to learn to apply. Failure on a problem may result from (a) not correctly comprehending the problem abstraction, (b) choosing the wrong abstraction, (c) incorrectly using the abstraction in the situation, or (d) incorrectly interpreting the results of using the abstraction in the situation. It is important to distinguish inability to comprehend. This may be easily determined by testing the extent to which the student is comprehending the situation before he attempts the application items. Determination of the point of failure as other than failure to comprehend (b, c, or d above) requires that a sufficient record of the student's problem-solving behavior be kept to allow location of the breakdown point. It is impossible and unnecessary for us to record every thought that occurs to the student in the solution of the problem. In general, it is sufficient to provide opportunity for the student to record his preference at each choice point in the solution to the problem through having him describe or actually record his thoughts at that point. If complete diagnosis is sought only on a few cases, having the student solve the problem aloud while an observer takes notes will get this information. If the cases are carefully chosen so as to be representative of the group, this latter technique will prove very feasible and economical for diagnosing the major troubles of the group as a whole. The technique is of great aid in the revision of the test items to make them more valid and to find choice points that should be recorded.

Providing opportunity for recording choice points sounds easy but is frequently very difficult in practice. Its implication is that we can anticipate all the correct as well as alternative problem-solving processes of the students. To avoid this, test constructors have tried to construct items which were so structured that by analyzing the student's answer one could infer the problem-solving process which the student used. That is, each distractor in a problem can be so phrased that it can be reached only by one set of problem-solving steps. By knowing the answer choice the student made we would then know the method he used to solve the problem. Verbal problem solving, in general, has shown that the types of items and variety of subject matter in which this technique can be successfully used are few. Although it may appear that the process can be inferred, studies usually show that students can come up with ways of arriving at answers, often correct, that no teacher seems to have anticipated. When accurate knowledge of process is required, actual recording of the student's problem-solving processes can be considered generally preferable in the majority of cases to inference from the product. [2]

---

[2] The recently developed "Tab Item" technique is an attempt to do this. In a letter to the editor, Robert Glaser has described the Tab Item:

"A Tab Item presents an examinee with the following: a description of a problem situation; a series of diagnostic procedures which, if employed, might yield information relevant to solving the problem; and a list of specific solutions, one of which is correct. In taking the test an examinee selects any number of the procedures presented which he thinks

Adequate sampling of application

We have stated that we wish to sample a student's behavior at several points in his application of abstraction to a problem situation but have not mentioned the obvious corollary that we should also sample the student's behavior over several problem situations. This is a general rule of testing and is another way of achieving what we commonly call "test reliability." It is, however, of particular importance with respect to application items. Since these items are often felt to be so difficult to construct, the use of a single problem situation to make generalizations about an individual is fairly common. Since the student's ability may often clearly be a function of the particular situation used, the necessity for taking a sample of situations is apparent.

---

will provide him with information necessary to solve the problem. The resulting information from whatever procedures the examinee chooses are given to him at the time he selects them. This is accomplished by giving the results or consequences of a procedure in the form of written or diagrammatic information, which is covered by a tab fastened to the page. When the examinee selects a procedure he rips off the tab and obtains the results of the procedure he has 'performed'. In a like manner an examinee is informed of the correctness or incorrectness of his choice of a solution. An examinee works on an item until he finds the correct solution, denoted by the word 'yes' under the corresponding tab."

Glaser, R.; Damrin, D. E.; and Gardner, F. M. "The Tab Item: A Technique for the Measurement of Proficiency in Diagnostic Problem Solving Tasks," Champaign: University of Illinois, College of Education, Bureau of Research and Service, June 1952.

Types of items illustrated

Major variations occur both in the kinds of situations posed, and in the extent and nature of the behavior requested in application items.

Behavior. The major variations in behavior involve variations in the extent to which the student is required to carry through the application process, and variations in the extent to which the student's problem-solving processes are recorded. These variations seem to occur most commonly in the following patterns:

Type

1) A recording of the choice of correct principle(s) is requested and its use in the problem is to be demonstrated. Practically the whole application process is on record.

2) The problem solution is requested and the process of application is to be demonstrated and recorded. The student's selection of the abstraction(s) is inferred from the nature of the process and solution he displays.

3) The complete or partial problem solution alone is requested and recorded. The selection and application of the abstraction(s) is entirely covert and unrecorded. They are inferred from the nature of the solution he presents. In some instances where only the solution is requested, if the solution is a complex one, it is sometimes difficult to determine whether the individual actually has applied the abstraction correctly so that the whole solution is correct. In these instances the extent of the student's solution and its correctness is sometimes explored by asking the student to indicate the implications of it.

4) Selection of the correct abstraction is alone requested
   and recorded. If a phenomenon is to be explained, the
   correct application of the abstraction is generally assumed to accompany a correct selection.   Although
   merely naming the abstraction is not usually a sufficient test of ability to use the abstraction correctly,
   problems requiring only the selection of the correct
   abstraction can be used when the abstraction and its
   application are simple and the problem's chief difficulty lies in selecting the correct abstraction.

Situation. As noted earlier, the emphasis in writing application items is on getting situations new to the student. This
is done by

Type

A) presenting a fictional situation,

B) using material with which the student is not likely
   to have had contact. Such situations are frequently
   simplified versions of complex material which
   would ordinarily come considerably later in the
   course of study (classification of an item as of
   this type is dependent entirely upon the group to
   whom it is administered),

C) taking a new slant on situations which to the group
   being tested are common and mundane.   In highly
   technical areas, "common" problems may appear
   very uncommon to an outsider.

3.00 - APPLICATION -- ILLUSTRATIVE TEST ITEMS

> **Behavior**. This adaptation of a PEA item requires the
> student to select the appropriate principles and extrap-
> olate beyond the situation given. The principle must
> be drawn from memory in this essay type item.
> (Type 1)
>
> **Situation**. The situation, while probably not within the
> direct experience of all, is at least within their vicari-
> ous experience. It could be considered as a new slant
> on a fairly common phenomenon. (Type C)

1. John prepared an aquarium as follows: He carefully cleaned a
ten-gallon glass tank with salt solution and put in a few inches of fine
washed sand. He rooted several stalks of weed (elodea) taken from a
pool and then filled the aquarium with tap water. After waiting a week
he stocked the aquarium with ten one-inch goldfish and three snails.
The aquarium was then left in a corner of the room. After a month
the water had not become foul and the plants and animals were in good
condition. Without moving the aquarium he sealed a glass top on it.

What prediction, if any, can be made concerning the condition of
the aquarium after a period of several months? If you believe a defi-
nite prediction can be made, make it and then give your reasons. If
you are unable to make a prediction for any reason, indicate why you
are unable to make a prediction (give your reasons).[3]

---

[3] Adapted from Test 1.3B, "Application of Principles in Science,"
Progressive Education Association, Evaluation in the Eight-Year
Study, University of Chicago, 1940.

132

Problem VI from PEA Test 1.3, Application of Principles

2. An electric iron (110 volts, 1000 watts) has been used for some time and the plug contacts have become burned, thus introducing additional resistance. How will this affect the amount of heat which the iron produces?

Directions: Choose the conclusion which you believe is most consistent with the facts given above and most reasonable in the light of whatever knowledge you may have, and mark the appropriate space on the Answer Sheet under Problem VI.

Conclusions:
A. The iron will produce more heat than when new.
B. The iron will produce the same heat as when new.
C. The iron will produce less heat than when new.

Directions: Choose the reasons you would use to explain or support your conclusion and fill in the appropriate spaces on your Answer Sheet. Be sure that your marks are in one column only--the same column in which you marked the conclusion.

Reasons:
1. The heat produced by an electrical device is always measured by its power rating. It is independent of any contact resistance.
2. Electric currents of the same voltage always produce the same amount of heat, and burned contacts do not decrease the amount of electricity entering the iron.
3. The current which flows through the iron is reduced when the resistance is increased.
4. Increasing the resistance in an electrical circuit increases the current.
5. An increase in electrical resistance increases the heat developed.
6. Manufacturers of electric irons urge that the contacts be kept clean to maintain maximum efficiency.
7. An increase in the temperature of a wire usually results in an increase in its resistance.
8. Burned contacts increase the heat developed in an electric iron just as increasing the friction in automobile brakes develops more heat.
9. The heat developed by an electric iron when connected to 110 volts is independent of the flow of current.

Behavior. In the following problem both the solution and process of application are requested. The student's correct selection of the abstraction, in this case a method of solving this type of problem, is inferred from the process and the solution he displays. (Type 2)

Situation. The problem situations are fictional and probably not realistic from the standpoint of most of the groups which would be tested. If this problem or one just like it had been solved in classwork, this would be a comprehension rather than an application item. (Type A)

3. X and Y can do a piece of work together in 15 days. They work together for 6 days; then X quits and Y finishes the work in 30 more days. In how many days can Y do the piece of work alone? Show your work below.

(a) 30
(b) 40
(c) 50
(d) 60
(e) none of the foregoing

Behavior. This item is similar to the preceding item in terms of the way that it tests application. In this instance the abstraction being tested is a formula relating the area to the length and width of a rectangle. (Type 2)

Situation. The problem is fictional. As noted in regard to the preceding item, if too close to the problems used in class, it would test comprehension rather than application. (Type A)

4. The length of a rectangular lot exceeds its breadth by 20 yards. If each dimension is increased by 20 yards the area of the lot will be doubled. Find the shorter dimension of the original lot. Show your work below.

(a) 20
(b) 30
(c) 35
(d) 40
(e) none of the foregoing

134

5. After the number on the answer sheet corresponding to that preceding each of the following paired items, blacken space
    A- if increase in the first of the things referred to is usually accompanied by increase in the second.
    B- if increase in the first of the things referred to is usually accompanied by decrease in the second.
    C- if increase in the first of the things referred to has no appreciable effect on the second.

  1. Number of lemming in an Arctic habitat.
     Number of caribou in the same habitat.

  2. Number of lichens in an Arctic habitat.
     Number of caribou in the same habitat.

  3. Amount of carbonates dissolved in the water of a river.
     Number of clams in the river.

  4. Temperature of the environment of a mammal.
     Body temperature of the mammal.

  5. Compactness of the soil of a given area.
     Amount of water absorption by the soil after a heavy rain.

  6. Frequency of fire in a given coniferous forest.
     Number of aspen trees in the forest.

  7. Crop yield per acre of farmland cultivated in Illinois.
     Amount of soil nutrients per acre of farmland.

  8. The altitude of the environment of an animal.
     Extent to which the circulating red blood cells of the animal undergo mitosis.

  9. Extent of tree planting activity on forest land in the United States.
     Degree of water absorption by the soil per unit of area of the same land.

  10. Amount of vegetation per square yard of soil.
     Amount of available nitrate salts in the same area of soil.

  11. Amount of humus accumulated in sand during dune succession.
     Abundance of animal life in the area.

Behavior. In this item the student is to judge the implications of applying a given policy for the distribution of income. The policy situation is given and the implication alone is asked for. The principles
involved and their use in determining the implications must be inferred from the student's choice. (Type 3)

Situation. The situation is fictional in that the setting of the problem
is abstract and the student is presented with a simplified economic
situation where only one variable at a time is changed. (Type A)

6. Directions: In the following items you are to judge the effects of a
particular policy on the distribution of income. In each case assume
that there are no other changes in policy which would counteract the effect of the policy described in the item. Mark the item:

A- if the policy described would tend to reduce the existing degree
of inequality in the distribution of income;
B- if the policy described would tend to increase the existing degree of inequality in the distribution of income; or
C- if the policy described would have no effect, or an indetermi-
nate effect, on the distribution of income.

Items:

_____ 1. Increasingly progressive income taxes.

_____ 2. Confiscation of rent on unimproved urban land.

_____ 3. Introduction of a national sales tax.

_____ 4. Increasing the personal exemptions from income taxes.

_____ 5. Distributing a subsidy to sharecroppers on Southern
farms.

_____ 6. Provision of educational and medical services, and low
cost public housing.

_____ 7. Reduction in the degree of business monopoly.

_____ 8. Increasing taxes in periods of prosperity and decreasing
them in periods when depressions threaten.

Behavior. The student is asked to find the solution. Correct selection and use of the appropriate principle is inferred from the solution. (Type 3)

Situation. Strictly a fictional situation, but having a realistic-sounding setting. (Type A)

---

7. Suppose an elevator is descending with a constant acceleration of gravity "g". If a passenger attempts to throw a rubber ball upward, what will be the motion of the ball with respect to the elevator? The ball will
    1. remain fixed at the point the passenger releases it.
    2. rise to the top of the elevator and remain there.
    3. not rise at all, but will fall to the floor.
    4. rise, bounce off the ceiling, then move toward the floor at a constant speed.
    5. rise, bounce off the ceiling, then move toward the floor at an increasing speed.

Behavior. Here one can test both the correct selection and use of the abstraction since the problem is to explain a phenomenon. (Type 4)

Situation. A common problem is used. (Type C)

Directions: The underlined statement at the end of the problem is assumed to be a correct answer. You are to explain the underlined conclusion by selecting statements from the list following the problem. (The student checks the explanations.)

8. If a person is planning to bathe in the sun, at what time of day is he most likely to receive a severe sunburn? He is most likely to receive a severe sunburn in the middle of the day (11 a.m. to 1 p.m.) because:
    ( ) We are slightly closer to the sun at noon than in the morning or afternoon.
    ( ) The noon sun will produce more "burn" than the morning or afternoon sun.
    ( ) When the sun's rays fall directly (straight down) on a surface, more energy is received by that surface than when the sun's rays fall obliquely on that surface.
    ( ) When the sun is directly overhead the sun's rays pass through less absorbing atmosphere than when the sun is lower in the sky.
    ( ) The air is usually warmer at noon than at other times of the day.
    ( ) The ultraviolet of the sunlight is mainly responsible for sunburn. [4]

---

[4] Taken from Inventory 1.5, Analyzing Health Problems; Cooperative Study in General Education. American Council on Education, University of Chicago, 1941.

> Behavior. The student must recall the principles of solar
> and planetary movement and apply them to each of the re-
> sponse possibilities to determine whether the problem sit-
> uation might be a resultant. Only the solution need be re-
> corded. (Type 3)
>
> Situation. Fictional. (Type A)

9. You have acquired some knowledge of the earth and its motions as
they really exist. In this exercise you are to identify the effects of
some wholly imaginary conditions. After each item number on the
answer sheet blacken space
   A- if the item would be true if the earth were not inclined on
       its axis.
   B- if the item would be true if the orbit of the earth were a circle
       rather than an ellipse.
   C- if the item would be true if the earth revolved toward the west
       rather than toward the east.
   D- if the item would be true if the earth had half its present diame-
       ter but retained its present mass.
   E- if the item would be true if the earth had no moon.

Assume only one of the above imaginary conditions occurs at a time.

1. All the solar days would be of equal length.

2. Objects would weigh four times as much as they do now.

3. The celestial equator and the ecliptic would be identical.

4. The sun would set in the east.

5. A different North Star would need to be chosen.

6. The force of gravity would be four times as great.

7. The orbital speed of the earth would not vary during the year.

8. We would know much less about the nature of the sun.

9. Night and day would be of equal length in all latitudes
    all year long.

When on Thursday, February 8, 1951 a Chicagoan, Mrs. Dorothy Mae Stevens, was found unconscious in a passageway after a night of exposure to 11 degree subzero weather, "she was literally frozen stiff."

Her temperature had dropped to an unprecedented 64 degrees (Fahrenheit). Twenty hours after her arrival at Michael Reese Hospital, her temperature had risen to 98.2 degrees. Early Friday it was 101 and later 100. On Saturday it was also 100.

When she was first found, her respiration was slowed to 3 a minute. By Saturday it was up to 24 a minute.

Her blood pressure was zero on Thursday. By Saturday it was 132 over 80. On Thursday her pulse rate was 12 a minute; on Saturday it was 100. Cortisone was administered early.

Behavior. This item requests solution and the principle used. (Type 1)

Situation. At the time the item was written Mrs. Stevens' case was headline news. The item assumes that the student has not previously thought about these aspects of the case. (Type C)

---

10. At a body temperature of 64 degrees

    A- the blood carries more oxygen to the cells than normally, because more gases dissolve in fluids at low temperatures rather than at high temperatures.
    B- the blood vessels of the skin are dilated, because the vasoconstrictor muscles are relaxed.
    C- the heart beats more rapidly, because the cold stimulates the heart center in the medulla.
    D- most activities slow down, because all chemical activities decrease as the temperature falls.

Behavior. Only the solution is requested, the abstraction used must be inferred from the student's choice. (Type 3)

Situation. See previous problem.

---

11. The immediate cause of Mrs. Stevens' unconsciousness was probably due to the

    A- lack of a sufficient amount of oxygen to the brain cells.
    B- lowering of the external temperature.
    C- slow pulse rate.
    D- decrease in muscle tone.
    E- low breathing rate.

Behavior. The solution alone is requested. (Type 3)

Situation. See first problem of this series.

12. When Mrs. Stevens was found in subzero weather her heart was beating

A- 12 times a minute.
B- 3 times a minute.
C- 0 times a minute.
D- the normal number of times a minute, but not with normal vigor.
E- subnormally, but there is nothing in the article to indicate how many times.

Behavior. The student must determine the principles involved in the production of steam which might apply to each of the distractors. He then determines whether this is realistic insofar as the situation is concerned. This leads him to a choice. An aspect of the solution is requested. (Type 3)

Situation. A realistic situation probably not previously considered by the student. (Type C)

After each exercise number on the answer sheet, blacken the <u>one</u> lettered space which designates the correct answer.

13. When a geyser first begins to erupt, hot water overflows at the orifice and this is followed by a rush of steam, mingled with hot water. The first overflow of hot water aids in the production of steam, because

A- less water needs to be heated.
B- more water can seep into the fissure from the surrounding rocks.
C- the higher the pressure, the greater the steam produced.
D- the lower the pressure, the lower the temperature at which steam is produced.
E- the water which overflows is necessarily below 212° F. in temperature.

Behavior. Proper application of the operating principles of certain bodily mechanisms permits the student to predict the direction and amount of change which will result from each of the two experiments. (Type 3)

Situation. This is a fictional experiment which is so devised that it permits the demonstration of certain principles. (Type A)

14.

Experiment A: A normal person is seated inside a small airtight chamber in which the air at the start of the experiment has a temperature of 72° F. and a relative humidity of 60. By means of a mask and pipes the person breathes air drawn in from outside the chamber and the air he exhales is also passed out of the chamber.

Experiment B: The same person is later seated outside of the same chamber, but by means of the mask and pipes breathes air drawn from the chamber and the air he exhales is also passed into the chamber. The composition of the air, air pressure, temperature, and humidity were the same outside and inside the chamber at the start of each of the experiments.

After each item number on the answer sheet, blacken space
   A- if the statement applies to Experiment A.
   B- if the statement applies to Experiment B.
   C- if the statement applies to neither Experiment A nor Experiment B.

The rate and depth of breathing increase more rapidly in this experiment than in the other experiment.

The rate and amount of perspiration increase more rapidly in this experiment than in the other experiment.

The humidity and temperature of the air in the chamber increase more rapidly in this experiment than in the other experiment.

The O_2 concentration of the air in the chamber increases appreciably.

The CO_2 concentration of the air in the chamber increases appreciably.

The percentage of heat loss through evaporation decreases greatly.

The activity of the respiratory center of the medulla increases considerably.

The activity of the respiratory center of the medulla decreases considerably.

The number of impulses passing through the phrenic nerves in a given unit of time increases considerably.

The number of impulses passing through the vagus nerves in a given unit of time increases considerably.

Behavior. The student must determine the general principles which
operate in the situation described and then predict the most likely
event. (Type 3)
Situation. A fictional situation. (Type A)

15. Mr. Golzak, Mr. A. F. Fell, Mrs. Hunter, and Boss Powers live
in Steel City.

Mr. Golzak was born 60 years ago in Central Europe. Today Mr. Golzak is one of Steel City's top business leaders. The Golzak family has
"arrived." Wealthy Mrs. Golzak dominates the social life of their
swank suburb, Mapledale. Mr. Golzak, personnel manager for Amalgamated Steel, believes in "rugged individualism." Personal freedom
allows enterprising men (such as himself) to achieve wealth and position, just as freedom from governmental restraint for business assures
national prosperity and a "full dinner pail" for all. Mr. Golzak believes
labor unions destroy workers' initiative and undermine business.

Mr. A. F. Fell was born in Steel City in a working-class neighborhood.
Like his father, Mr. Fell became a printer's apprentice at 16, and
then a life-long member of the International Typographical Workers
Union. He works as a typesetter for the "Steel City Sentinel." Mr. Fell
believes that management and labor should settle their differences entirely between themselves by collective bargaining. Mr. Fell makes
$1.90 per hour, owns his own home and sends his children to the city
junior college. He believes his union has made this possible.

Mrs. Hunter is the wife of a steel workers. Mr. Hunter belongs to the
CIO. The Hunters and three other families share a "modest" home
(owned by Mr. Golzak) three blocks downwind from the steel mill. Mrs.
Hunter attended a Southern school for Negroes for four years, off and
on. She has little understanding of social and economic problems, but
she worries over such personal problems as clothing for four growing
children, privacy in her own home, paying the butcher during the steel
strike, and Junior who "borrows" bicycles.

Boss Powers, slum-born son of an Irish saloon-keeper, learned con-
viviality early in life and led his gang against the Prairie Avenue Dukes.
Soon he was leading his Ward Organization against the Republicans.
Today he is unquestioned as Democratic Boss of Steel City. He enjoys
the fruits of victory.

1. A business recession would probably mean unemployment for
(A- the Fells and the Hunters; B- Boss Powers; C- the Hunters;
D- none of these).

2. Mr. Fell's home is probably (A- near the steel mill; B- in Mapledale; C- in the zone of transition; D- among twenty-year-old
single dwelling units).

3. A bill is before Congress to admit an additional 100,000 displaced
persons. Most likely to favor the bill is (A- Mr. Golzak, personnel
manager for Amalgamated Steel; B- Mrs. Hunter, wife of an unskilled laborer; C- Mr. Fell, skilled craftsman; D- Boss Powers,
son of an immigrant).

4. Mrs. Fell has chronic headaches although her doctor can find nothing organically wrong with her. Her headaches are most probably
a result of (A- personal maladjustment; B- approaching insanity;
C- hidden germs; D- an inherited mental weakness).

Behavior. The student must apply the physics principle correctly in each case. Only the solution is requested. (Type 3)

Situation. Fictional. (Type A)

16. The numbers preceding the paired items in the exercise below refer to the corresponding numbers on the answer sheet. Considering each pair from the standpoint of quantity, blacken space

    A- if the item at the left is greater than that at the right.

    B- if the item at the right is greater than that at the left.

    C- if the two items are of essentially the same magnitude.

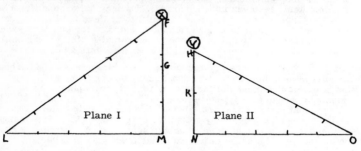

Two spheres, X and Y, of equal masses and radii, are placed on two inclined planes, as shown in the diagram. Neglect friction and air resistance, and assume that potential energy is measured from the level of points L, M, N, and O.

1. Potential energy of X at F .... Potential energy of Y at H.
2. Potential energy of X at M .... Potential energy of Y at N.
3. Potential energy of X at M .... Potential energy of X at L.
4. Kinetic energy of X on rolling to L .. Kinetic energy of X on falling to M.
5. Kinetic energy of X on rolling to L .. Kinetic energy of Y on rolling to O.
6. Work done on X in raising it from M to F .... Work done on X in moving it from L to F.
7. Work done on X in raising it from M to F .... Work done on Y in raising it from N to H.
8. Acceleration of X in rolling down incline toward L................ Acceleration of Y in rolling down incline toward O.
9. Acceleration of X in falling vertically toward M .... Acceleration of Y in falling vertically toward N.
10. Time it takes X to fall to M .... Time it takes Y to fall to N.
11. Time it takes X to roll to L .... Time it takes X to fall to M.
12. Loss of potential energy of X in falling to G .... Loss of potential energy of Y in falling to K.

Behavior. The student must recall the general principles of supply and demand and determine their use in each situation to determine the effect of the situation. Solution only is requested. (Type 3)

Situation. Fictional situations which exemplify the points involved. (Type A)

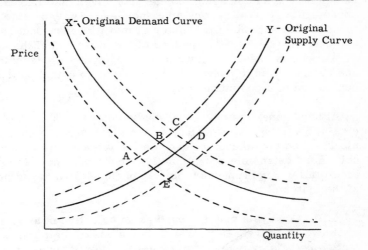

17. In the diagram above the unbroken lines represent the original supply and demand condition for each of the products listed below. For each product a change of conditions is specified which may cause a shift in either or both of the original curves, such that the new point of intersection is at A, B, C, D, or E. (B and D represent shifts in demand or supply, but not both, while A, C, and E represent a shift in both supply and demand.)

After the answer sheet number which precedes each product, blacken the lettered space which designates the point of intersection of the curves which apply to the new conditions. Assume that there are no other changes in supply or demand than those specified. Assume also that there are no restrictions which interfere with the existence of a free market.

Product	New Conditions
1. Automobiles	New union agreements have practically eliminated labor grievances. Those who most urgently wanted new cars have been supplied.
2. Butter	During the winter months production is lowest. Taxes on oleomargarine have been eliminated.
3. Shoes	Stockmen are holding back beef cattle from the market in anticipation of higher prices.
4. Oysters	The Chesapeake Bay oysters are found to be succumbing to sicknesses induced by increasing pollution of the bay.

4.00 - ANALYSIS

At a somewhat more advanced level than the skills of comprehension and application are those involved in analysis. In comprehension the emphasis is on the grasp of the meaning and intent of the material. In application it is on remembering and bringing to bear upon given material the appropriate generalizations or principles. Analysis emphasizes the breakdown of the material into its constituent parts and detection of the relationships of the parts and of the way they are organized. It may also be directed at the techniques and devices used to convey the meaning or to establish the conclusion of a communication.

Although analysis may be conducted merely as an exercise in detecting the organization and structure of a communication and may therefore become its own end, it is probably more defensible educationally to consider analysis as an aid to fuller comprehension or as a prelude to an evaluation of the material.

Skill in analysis may be found as an objective of any field of study. It is frequently expressed as one of their important objectives by teachers of science, social studies, philosophy, and the arts. They wish, for example, to develop in students the ability to distinguish fact from hypothesis in a communication, to identify conclusions and supporting statements, to distinguish relevant from extraneous material, to note how one idea relates to another, to see what unstated assumptions are involved in what is said, to distinguish dominant from subordinate ideas or themes in poetry or music, to find evidence of the author's techniques and purposes, etc., etc.

No entirely clear lines can be drawn between analysis and comprehension at one end or between analysis and evaluation at the other. Comprehension deals with the content of material, analysis with both content and form. One may speak of "analyzing" the meaning of a communication, but this usually refers to a more complex level of ability than "understanding" or "comprehending" the meaning -- and that is the intention in the use of "analysis" here. It is true also that analysis shades into evaluation, especially when we think of "critical analysis." As one analyzes the relationships of elements

of an argument, he may be judging how well the argument
hangs together. In analyzing the form of a communication,
or the techniques used, one may express opinions about how
well the communication serves its purpose.

And yet the type of ability we call analysis may be ab-
stracted, and usefully. One who comprehends the meaning
of a communication may not be able to analyze it at all effectively, and one who is skillful in the analysis of material
may evaluate it badly. In the selection of the illustrative educational objectives and test items which follow, an attempt
has been made to use materials clearly above the level of
comprehension and below that of evaluation.

Analysis, as an objective, may be divided into three
types or levels. At one level the student is expected to
break down the material into its constituent parts, to identify or classify the elements of the communication. At a second level he is required to make explicit the relationships
among the elements, to determine their connections and interactions. A third level involves recognition of the organizational principles, the arrangement and structure, which
hold together the communication as a whole.

4.10 - Analysis of Elements

A communication may be conceived of as composed of a
large number of elements. Some of these elements are explicitly stated or contained in the communication and can be
recognized and classified relatively easily. Thus, the reader of a communication should have little difficulty in recognizing the hypotheses which are being investigated since they
are likely to be so identified by the writer. He may also be
able to recognize the conclusions the writer is drawing because these are also likely to be stated explicitly by the
writer.

However, there are many other elements in a communication which are not so clearly labelled or identified by the
writer. Many of these elements may be of paramount importance in determining the nature of the communication, and
until the reader can detect them he may have difficulty in
fully comprehending or evaluating the communication. Thus
there are unstated assumptions being made by the writer

which can only be inferred from an analysis of a series of statements within the document. It is also of value to the reader if he can detect the nature and function of particular statements in the communication. Some are statements of fact, some are statements of value, while others may be statements of intent. Many other types of statements may be included and it is left to the reader to determine the nature of each.

4.10 - <u>Analysis of Elements</u>--Illustrative Educational Objectives

The ability to recognize unstated assumptions.

Skill in distinguishing facts from hypotheses.

The ability to distinguish factual from normative statements.

Skill in identifying motives and in discriminating between mechanisms of behavior with reference to individuals and groups.

Ability to distinguish a conclusion from statements which support it.

4.20 - <u>Analysis of Relationships</u>

Having identified the different elements within a communication, the reader still has the task of determining some of the major relationships among the elements as well as the relationships among the various parts of the communication. At the most obvious level he may need to determine the relationship of the hypotheses to the evidence, and in turn the relationship between the conclusions and the hypotheses as well as evidence. Analysis would also include the relationships among the different kinds of evidence presented.

At a more difficult level is likely to be the analysis of a communication into the parts which are essential to or which form the main thesis as contrasted with those parts or elements which may help to expand, develop, or support this thesis. Much of analysis of relationships may deal with the consistency of part to part, or element to element; or the relevance of elements or parts to the central idea or thesis in the communication.

4.20 - Analysis of Relationships--Illustrative Educational Objectives

Skill in comprehending the interrelationships among the ideas in a passage.

Ability to recognize what particulars are relevant to the validation of a judgment.

Ability to recognize which facts or assumptions are essential to a main thesis or to the argument in support of that thesis.

Ability to check the consistency of hypotheses with given information and assumptions.

Ability to distinguish cause-and-effect relationships from other sequential relationships.

Ability to analyze the relations of statements in an argument, to distinguish relevant from irrelevant statements.

Ability to detect logical fallacies in arguments.

Ability to recognize the causal relations and the important and unimportant details in an historical account.

4.30 - Analysis of Organizational Principles

At an even more complex and difficult level is likely to be the task of analyzing the structure and organization of a communication. Rarely will the producer of a communication explicitly point out the organizational principles he has used and quite frequently he may not be aware of the principles he has utilized. Thus, his purpose, point of view, attitude, or general conception of a field may be discerned in the writing and the reader may be unable to fully comprehend or evaluate the communication until he has determined them.

Similarly, the producer of a communication selects some form, pattern, or structure and organizes his arguments, evidence, or other elements around these. The analysis of these underlying organizational qualities should help in the comprehension as well as evaluation of the entire communication. Frequently it is impossible to make an evaluation until this has been done.

4.30 - <u>Analysis of Organizational Principles</u>--Illustrative Educational Objectives

Ability to analyze, in a particular work of art, the relation of materials and means of production to the "elements" and to the organization.

The ability to recognize form and pattern in literary or artistic works as a means of understanding their meaning.

The ability to infer the author's purpose, point of view, or traits of thought and feeling as exhibited in his work.

Ability to infer an author's concept of science, philosophy, history, or of his art as exemplified in his practice.

Ability to see the techniques used in persuasive materials, such as advertising, propaganda, etc.

Ability to recognize the point of view or bias of a writer in an historical account.

Testing for Analysis, and illustrative test items

In testing the ability to analyze, the student may be asked questions about some material with which he is presumed to be familiar, or the material for analysis may be presented to him in the test situation. His ability to analyze material is usually tested more dependably in the latter case, for then one can be more confident that his answers are not affected by lack of familiarity with the material or inability to remember it adequately. While it is true that knowledge is used, and is often required, in making an adequate analysis of any communication, there are few occasions when one must analyze material without having that material before him. If the material to be analyzed is new to the student, and appropriate questions are used, it is likely to be a genuine test of his analytical abilities, for he has no opportunity to use analytical comments which he simply recalls from previous discussions of the material.

The material given for analysis in a test may be a literary passage, a description of a scientific experiment or a social situation, a set of data, an argument, a picture, a musical selection, etc., etc. Or the student may be placed in an actual situation, such as a laboratory in which he analyzes the reactions of materials, or a classroom in which he must analyze the interactions of members of the group, or-- as is well known in military training and testing--a field situation in which he must identify and relate a variety of factors.

The student may show his ability by making a series of free or guided responses, or by selecting the best answers to objective questions. An advantage of the latter method is that items can be structured so that the answers include common errors which students are likely to make.

The errors in analysis may be grouped as follows:

A. Crude errors

> Misjudging the nature of elements of the communication or the relationships between elements. Confusing basic and subordinate elements.

Inability to identify forms and patterns. Failure to see the bearing of elements upon the intent of the communication as a whole.

B. Incomplete analysis

The student may be essentially "on the right track," but he misses some of the elements, relationships, or principles which he ought to see.

C. Over-analysis

Some students go too far in their effort to analyze a communication, breaking it up into more minute elements than is appropriate for the given material, and thereby often missing the more important relationships.

D. Other limited errors

Test items may be so structured that several answers are partly right but one represents a more adequate analysis than the others. Here the distinction is not between right and wrong, or between ability and inability, but is made in terms of the quality of analysis.

4.00 - ANALYSIS -- ILLUSTRATIVE TEST ITEMS

4.10 - <u>Analysis of Elements</u>

> In Items 1 - 9 each item requires students to identify an element of a communication. No. 8 asks for an "important" unstated assumption, which would seem to involve analysis of relationships; actually, however, all except one of the answers presented in the item are either stated or <u>not</u> assumed, so that the student has only to identify the one answer which represents an unstated assumption.

1. Galileo investigated the problem of the acceleration of falling bodies by rolling balls down very smooth planes inclined at increasing angles, since he had no means of determining very short intervals of time. From the data obtained he extrapolated for the case of free fall. Which of the following is an assumption implicit in the extrapolation?

    1. That air resistance is negligible in free fall.
    2. That objects fall with constant acceleration.
    3. That the acceleration observed with the inclined plane is the same as that involved in free fall.
    4. That the planes are frictionless.
    5. That a vertical plane and one which is nearly so have nearly the same effect on the ball.

2. A and B were arguing about the desirability of adopting a nationwide system of compulsory health insurance in the United States. B said that, while he had no fundamental objection to health insurance, he felt strongly that people should not be compelled to participate in it. "Now, look here," he said, "Do the people want health insurance or don't they? I don't think they do, but in either case, compulsory insurance is bad. If the people really want health insurance, there is no need for compulsion. If they don't want it, it is impossible to force them to participate. And so the answer is clear."

    Which of the following statements most nearly expresses the logical conclusion of B's argument?

    1. Health insurance is bad.
    2. Compulsory health insurance is bad.
    3. Compulsion is impossible.
    4. Compulsion is unnecessary.
    5. Compulsion is either unnecessary or impossible.

152

(Item 3 accompanies a reading passage in the test booklet.)

3. Which of the following is an assumption, specific to this experiment, that was made in the determination of the charge?

    1. The force of gravity is the same whether the drops are charged or not.
    2. Opposite charges attract each other.
    3. Only a single charge is present on a drop.
    4. The mass of a drop is equal to its density times its volume.
    5. None of these.

Items 4 and 5 refer to the following paragraph:

> "For what men say is that, if I am really just and am not
> 2 also thought just, profit there is none, but the pain and loss
> on the other hand is unmistakable. But if, though unjust, I
> 4 acquire the reputation of justice, a heavenly life is promised
> to me. Since then appearance tyrannizes over truth and is lord
> 6 of happiness, to appearance I must devote myself. I will describe around me a picture and shadow of virtue to be the
> 8 vestibule and exterior of my house; behind I will trail the
> subtle and crafty fox."

4. Which one of the following best states the major premise of the argument?

    1. "For what men say is" (line 1).
    2. "if I am really just" (line 1).
    3. "profit there is none" (line 2).
    4. "appearance tyrannizes over truth and is lord of happiness" (line 5).
    5. "to appearance I must devote myself" (line 6).

5. Which one of the following best states the conclusion of the argument?

    1. "For what men say is" (line 1).
    2. "if I am really just" (line 1)
    3. "profit there is none" (line 2).
    4. "appearance tyrannizes over truth and is lord of happiness" (line 5).
    5. "to appearance I must devote myself" (line 6).

(Other items, involving analysis of relationships, can be based on this same paragraph. See Item 17, below.)

Item 6 refers to the following situation:

The college committee in charge of social regulations was holding an open hearing on a proposal that the rule on chaperoning coeducational outings (wiener roasts, overnight hikes, campfires, etc.) should be more strictly applied. A student in the audience got the floor and made this speech:

(A) This whole discussion is ridiculous,
(B) for we shouldn't have chaperones at all!
(C) You see, any chaperone you get will either arrange not to see what happens or he will be so badly outnumbered he can't keep track of what is going on.
(D) But chaperones are supposed to guarantee that what goes on is respectable.
(E) So the chaperonage system is utterly ineffective and full of hypocrisy.
(F) Besides, collegians will never develop maturity unless they are given responsibilities to exercise and are really trusted with these responsibilities.

6. There is one statement in the student's argument for which reasons are offered, but which he does not offer as a reason for any other statement. That statement, his main conclusion, is

1. A.   4. E.
2. B.   5. F.
3. C.

(The following question is based on an excerpt from Lindsay, The Modern Democratic State, which was distributed prior to the examination and students were permitted to refer to the book and to any notes during the examination.)

7. The main question that Lindsay attempts to answer in Chapter I is:

1. What is the sovereign authority in the state?
2. What is the relation of law to sovereignty?
3. What is the relation of authority and consent to sovereignty?
4. Is sovereignty advisable?

Items 8 and 9 refer to the following situation:

A group of college students were discussing the relative merits of two grading systems. It had been suggested that only two grades be used: S (satisfactory) and U (unsatisfactory), instead of the A-B-C-D-F system then in use at the college. One student made the following statement:

"People go to college to learn, not just to get grades. Grades are no indication of absolute degree of learning, they are purely relative and then mostly determined by chance or probability (guessing, multiple-choice tests, etc.). The student is a better judge of how he is doing than the professor. Therefore, an S-U system would be better since it would cut down the amount of differentiation between grades and give a better picture of how the student is doing."

8. An important unstated assumption involved in this argument is that

    1. the accuracy of the A-B-C-D-F system cannot or will not be significantly improved.
    2. people go to college to learn.
    3. the student is a better judge of how he is doing than the professor.
    4. an S-U system would be better.
    5. grades have no importance.

9. The conclusion of this student's argument is that

    1. grades should be abolished.
    2. students do not care about their grades.
    3. students should grade themselves.
    4. a new grading system should be substituted for the present one.
    5. the present grading system is better than the proposed substitute.

    (Other items, involving analysis of relationships, can be based on this same situation. See Items 18 and 19, below.)

4.20 - <u>Analysis of Relationships</u>

> Items 10 and 11 call for analysis of the relation-
> ships of statements in an argument. They accom-
> pany Item 6 in a test.

Items 10 and 11 refer to the following situation:

The college committee in charge of social regulations was holding
an open meeting on a proposal that the rule on chaperoning coeducational outings (wiener roasts, overnight hikes, campfires, etc.)
should be more strictly applied. A student in the audience got the
floor and made this speech:

(A) This whole discussion is ridiculous,
(B) for we shouldn't have chaperones at all!
(C) You see, any chaperone you get will either arrange not to
    see what happens or he will be so badly outnumbered he
    can't keep track of what is going on.
(D) But chaperones are supposed to guarantee that what goes
    on is respectable.
(E) So the chaperonage system is utterly ineffective and full
    of hypocrisy.
(F) Besides, collegians will never develop maturity unless
    they are given responsibilities to exercise and are really
    trusted with these responsibilities.

10. The student offered <u>A</u> as a reason for

    1. B.
    2. C.
    3. D.
    4. E.
    5. None of these.

11. The student offered <u>B</u> as a reason for

    1. A.
    2. C.
    3. D.
    4. E.
    5. None of these.

(Similar items refer to statements C, D, E, and F.)

156

Items 12 - 14 require students to interpret the quoted
statement and to analyze the relations of elements of
the statement and of the play to the general import of
the statement. Items 12 and 13 involve analysis in
terms of relevance; Item 14 involves analysis in terms
of consistency.

Items 12 to 14 are based on the following paragraph:

"(1) Hamlet is given a command by the ghost of his murdered father
to take vengeance upon the murderer, Claudius. (2) He is not able
to do so immediately because he does not have sufficient proof that
Claudius has murdered his father. (3) In the process of finding this
proof, Hamlet unwittingly allows the king to discover his suspicions.
(4) As the action proceeds, Hamlet cannot take vengeance because he
never has a real opportunity to do so. (5) As the action ends, Hamlet becomes involved in a duel arranged by Claudius which has as its
consequence the death of the hero and his adversary as well as the
more important of the subordinate characters."

12. A discussion and evaluation of the statement given above would
    revolve most around the points made in
    1. sentence 1.
    2. sentences 2 and 3.
    3. sentences 2 and 4.
    4. sentence 5.

13. Assume, temporarily, complete agreement with the statement.
    In discussing various parts of the play, which among the follow-
    ing would you tend to minimize?

    1. Hamlet's interview with the ghost in Act I.
    2. The lapse of time between Acts I and II.
    3. The play within the play.
    4. Hamlet's departure for England.
    5. The short lapse of time between the play within the play
       and Hamlet's departure for England.

14. Which of the following statements about Hamlet is least incon-
    sistent with the general position taken in the statement?

    1. Hamlet is a man of action.
    2. Hamlet is by nature a meditative person, not accustomed
       to meet problems by direct action.
    3. Hamlet is an intellectual, over whom someone more shrewd
       even if less learned has the advantage in the world of prac-
       tical affairs.
    4. Hamlet is normally a sensitive, good-natured person, who,
       however, during the period covered by the first four acts
       of the play, is in a state of melancholy -- a condition in-
       duced by his father's death and accompanied by a great
       lethargy.

Items 15 and 16 are designed to test such an objective as "ability to recognize which facts or assumptions are essential to a main thesis or to the argument in support of that thesis." Item 16 accompanies Item 3 in a test.

15. Statement of facts: The following table represents the relationship between the yearly income of certain families and the medical attention they receive.

Family Income	Per Cent of Family Members Who Received No Medical Attention During the Year
Under $1,200	47
$1,200 to $3,000	40
$3,000 to $5,000	33
$5,000 to $10,000	24
Over $10,000	14

Conclusion: Members of families with small incomes are healthier than members of families with large incomes.

Which one of the following assumptions would be necessary to justify the conclusion?

1. Wealthy families had more money to spend for medical care.
2. All members of families who needed medical attention received it.
3. Many members of families with low incomes were not able to pay their doctor bills.
4. Members of families with low incomes often did not receive medical attention.

(Item 16 accompanies a reading passage in the test booklet.)

16. Which of the following assumptions is necessary in order to determine the mass of a drop by the method described?

1. The drop falls with uniform acceleration.
2. All the drops sprayed into the chamber are of the same size.
3. The drop is charged.
4. The drop is nearly spherical.
5. The electrical force is equal to the gravitational force.

Item 17, calling for analysis of the way one element functions in relation to others, accompanies Items 4 and 5 in a test.

Item 17 refers to the following paragraph:

"For what men say is that, if I am really just and am not also
2   thought just, profit there is none, but the pain and loss on the
    other hand is unmistakable. But if, though unjust, I acquire
4   the reputation of justice, a heavenly life is promised to me.
    Since then appearance tyrannizes over truth and is lord of hap-
6   piness, to appearance I must devote myself. I will describe
    around me a picture and shadow of virtue to be the vestibule
8   and exterior of my house; behind I will trail the subtle and
    crafty fox."

17. What is the function of the last sentence (lines 6-9)? The sentence

    1. restates the central thesis in figurative language.
    2. advances the premise of the argument.
    3. presents factual data to support the central thesis.
    4. contradicts the central thesis.
    5. introduces a new concept.

Items 18 and 19 require analysis of the relevance and importance of elements in an argument. They accompany Items 8 and 9 in a test.

Items 18 and 19 refer to the following situation:

A group of college students were discussing the relative merits of two grading systems. It had been suggested that only two grades be used: S (satisfactory) and U (unsatisfactory), instead of the A-B-C-D-F system then in use at the college. One student made the following statement:

"People go to college to learn, not just to get grades. Grades are no indication of absolute degree of learning, they are purely relative and then mostly determined by chance or probability (guessing, multiple-choice tests, etc.). The student is a better judge of how he is doing than the professor. Therefore, an S-U system would be better since it would cut down the amount of differentiation between grades and give a better picture of how the student is doing."

18. The conclusion depends fundamentally on the proposition that

    1. people do not go to college just to get grades.
    2. the student is the best judge of how he is doing.
    3. grades are very inaccurate indications of what students have learned.
    4. one grading system is better than the other.
    5. multiple-choice tests are used in determining grades.

19. Which of the following statements is <u>least</u> essential as a part of the argument?

    1. Grades are no indication of absolute degree of learning.
    2. An S-U system would cut down the amount of differentiation between grades.
    3. An S-U system would give a better picture of how the student is doing.
    4. Grades are determined by chance or probability.
    5. The student is a better judge of how he is doing than the professor.

> Items 20 and 21 are based on an excerpt from Lindsay's <u>The Modern Democratic State</u> and accompany Item 7 in a test. These two items call for analysis of relationships between elements of a communication. Note that No. 20 requires, not merely the identification of an element (assumption), but a judgment concerning what assumption is essential in relation to other elements.

20. An assumption basic to Lindsay's preference for voluntary associations rather than government orders (Paragraph 73) is a belief

    1. that government is not organized to make the best use of experts.
    2. that freedom of speech, freedom of meeting, freedom of association, are possible only under a system of voluntary associations.
    3. in the value of experiment and initiative as a means of attaining an ever-improving society.
    4. in the benefits of competition.

21. The relation between the definition of sovereignty given in Paragraph 2 and that given in Paragraph 9 is best expressed as follows:

    1. There is no fundamental difference between them, only a difference in formulation.
    2. The definition given in Paragraph 2 includes that given in Paragraph 9, but in addition includes situations which are excluded by that given in Paragraph 9.
    3. The definition given in Paragraph 9 includes that given in Paragraph 2, but in addition includes situations which are excluded by that given in Paragraph 2.
    4. The two definitions are incompatible with each other; the conditions of sovereignty implied in each exclude the other.

> The following group of items is designed to test the
> objective: "Ability to recognize what particulars
> are relevant to the validation of a judgment."

Items 22 to 26 are to be judged in relation to this resolution:

Resolved: <u>That the term of the President of the United States
should be extended to six years</u>.

Some statements in Items 22 to 26 support the resolution, either directly or indirectly, some could be used in arguing against the resolution, and some have no bearing on the issue at all. Mark each
statement

    A. if you feel that it could be used by the affirmative side in a
       debate on the resolution.
    N. if you feel that it could be used by the negative side.
    X. if you feel it has no bearing on either side of the argument.

    (NOTE: You are not asked to judge the truth or falsity of the
             resolution or the statements.)

22. Efficiency increases with experience.

23. According to the principles upon which the United States was
    founded, the people should have a frequent check on the Presi-
    dent.

24. The party system has many disadvantages.

25. During most of a presidential election year the economic life
    of the nation is depressed by the uncertainty as to the outcome.

26. The people should have the opportunity to keep a satisfactory
    President as long as they wish.

4.30 - Analysis of Organizational Principles

> The following question relates to a selection given in
> the test. Students cannot answer this question sim-
> ply by finding a statement which is true of the article
> to which the item refers. They must judge which state-
> ment best expresses the purport of the article as a
> whole; this requires analysis of the organization and
> structure of the entire communication.

27. Which one of the following is the best description of the article
    as a whole?

    1. It presents historical evidence to prove what a govern-
       ment of equal rights is like.
    2. It presents evidence that policies pursued in the past have
       not been consistent with the ideal of a government of equal
       rights.
    3. It presents arguments to show that certain policies pur-
       sued in the past are undesirable.
    4. It is an effort to define the true functions of government.

> Items 28 and 29 are based on a composition which is
> played during the test. No. 28 calls for analysis of the
> systematic arrangement or structure which makes the
> composition a unit. No. 29 tests such an objective as
> "ability to analyze, in a particular work of art, the re-
> lation of materials and means of production to the
> 'elements' and to the organization."

28. The general structure of the composition is

    1. theme and variations.
    2. theme, development, restatement.
    3. theme 1, development; theme 2, development.
    4. introduction, theme, development.

29. The theme is carried essentially by

    1. the strings.
    2. the woodwinds.
    3. the horns.
    4. all in turn.

5.00 -- SYNTHESIS

Synthesis is here defined as the putting together of elements and parts so as to form a whole. This is a process of working with elements, parts, etc., and combining them in such a way as to constitute a pattern or structure not clearly there before. Generally this would involve a recombination of parts of previous experience with new material, reconstructed into a new and more or less well-integrated whole. This is the category in the cognitive domain which most clearly provides for creative behavior on the part of the learner. However, it should be emphasized that this is not completely free creative expression since generally the student is expected to work within the limits set by particular problems, materials, or some theoretical and methodological framework.

Comprehension, application, and analysis also involve the putting together of elements and the construction of meanings, but these tend to be more partial and less complete than synthesis in the magnitude of the task. Also there is less emphasis upon uniqueness and originality in these other classes than in the one under discussion here. Perhaps the main difference between these categories and synthesis lies in the possibility that they involve working with a given set of materials or elements which constitutes a whole in itself. They involve studying a whole in order to understand it better. In synthesis, on the other hand, the student must draw upon elements from many sources and put these together into a structure or pattern not clearly there before. His efforts should yield a product--something that can be observed through one or more of the senses and which is clearly more than the materials he began to work with. It is to be expected that a problem which is classified as a task primarily involving synthesis will also require all of the previous categories to some extent.

We recognize the difficulty of classifying essay questions. The tendency is to place them in the synthesis category. For example, if the student writes out his comprehension or analysis of a reading selection, does such a form of response constitute synthesis as we have defined it? If his essay involves analysis in terms of underlying elements and the like, perhaps not, since he has not come out with a product substantially different from that which he is studying.

162

If we accept this point of view, then we would not regard every act of writing as an act of synthesis. We would assume that writing as such is primarily a skill in expression, much of which represents the remembering of ideas, the interpretation of given materials, and the translation of ideas into writing.

For the present, it seems best to distinguish between different kinds of synthesis primarily on the basis of the product. Such an approach does permit classification into three relatively distinct divisions which have some practical significance. Classification on the basis of product is not inconsistent with the taxonomy, since the construction of different products may well require somewhat different processes. A similar assumption is made in the Knowledge and Analysis categories of this Handbook.

In the first sub-category, one may view the product or performance as essentially a unique communication. Usually the author is trying to communicate certain ideas and experiences to others, but in some instances he may be interested in expression for its own sake. Usually too he tries to communicate for one or more of the following purposes--to inform, to describe, to persuade, to impress, or to entertain. Ultimately, he wishes to achieve a given effect (response) in some audience. Consequently, he uses a particular medium of expression, together with its forms and conventions, to organize certain ideas and experiences. The product, or outcome of the synthesis, can be considered "unique" in at least two respects. First, it does not represent a proposed set of operations or specifications to be carried out, except perhaps in the narrow sense of furnishing an expressive design which may be interpreted and performed by an individual or group, as in the reading aloud of poetry, the presentation of a play, or the performance of a musical composition. Secondly, it does not ordinarily represent a contribution to our fund of tested knowledge; in fact, its relation to an external theoretical structure is not at issue.

In the second sub-category, one may view the product as a plan or proposed set of operations to be carried out. This may be illustrated as follows:

Proposed set of operations	Process—i.e., carrying out the set of operations	Expected outcome
Plan for an experiment	Carrying out the experiment	Experimental findings; probability statement
A teaching unit	Teaching	Changes in behavior
Specifications for a new house	Building the house	The house

The products of synthesis classified here thus fall in the first column. Clearly, each represents a kind of communication in the sense that a particular author or worker is trying to tell somebody something and has recorded his ideas (in rare instances he may carry these ideas around in his head and we then have to infer them from his process of carrying them out). But these efforts represent more than communication in the sense just outlined. They represent an attempt to propose a set of operations. In this sense, products that fall in this group are incomplete; until they are translated into action they represent mere ideas. Ordinarily, products of synthesis that fall in this second group must meet a set of fairly rigorous objective criteria.

In the third sub-category, one may view the product of synthesis as primarily a set of abstract relations. The set of relations may be derived from an analysis of certain observed phenomena, in which case they may be considered possible relations, or hypotheses to be tested; or they may be derived from an analysis of relations among propositions or other symbolic representations, in which case they may be considered necessary relations, or deductions. The distinguishing feature of this sub-category is thus the attempt to derive abstract relations from a detailed analysis. The relations themselves are not explicit from the start; they must be discovered or deduced.

Related concepts and processes. Since certain other concepts and processes overlap with the synthesis category, we will discuss them briefly. One of these is the phenomenon of central organization in which the brain and nervous system act as a vast organizing system. Some stimuli become focal in consciousness, and are perceived as "figure"; others remain peripheral and become part of the background; still others remain out of consciousness entirely. In a very real way, central organization represents a synthetic act. Because of its very pervasiveness, however, it would not help us draw distinctions among different forms of cognitive behavior. The same would be true of the process of "integration," the notion that every experience involves a combination of parts of previous experience with the present experience in such a way that the organism is permanently changed, however slightly.

Often the concept of integration is discussed in terms of "creative learning." This raises the philosophical question of whether or not all learning is "creative." In one sense, all learning is creative; the individual has acquired an understanding or some other reorganization of experience which is novel for him. The novelty for him is what makes the experience "creative." Many psychologists and educators would argue similarly, and certainly this view would be consistent with the theoretical framework of this taxonomy. Other writers, particularly sociologists and anthropologists, would prefer restricting the meaning of "creativity" to the production of something new, unique, and original in man's culture--the traditional meaning.

A concept related to "creative learning" is that of "creative expression." The latter concept usually refers to a type of education which encourages self-expression on the part of the learner. Rich sensory experience and freedom to express one's whole personality are considered basic conditions. Although literature, fine arts, music, and drama seem to be the most popular media, creative expression need not be limited to these. Such activities represent synthetic processes to the extent that they require the individual to organize ideas into new patterns, and probably many of them do. However, many do not qualify because they emphasize expression of emotional impulses and physical movements, rather than organization of ideas. Probably the main difference between "synthesis" and "creative expression" lies in the greater inclusiveness of the latter term. Whether all efforts at synthesis shall be considered "creative expression," however, would not seem immediately evident. Much would depend on the nature of the individual's motivation and how freely he gave himself to the task.

Educational significance of synthesis objectives. Philosophical arguments for the cultivation of synthesis objectives are numerous and need not be documented here.
Typically, they emphasize personal expression as against
passive participation, and independence of thought and action
as against dependence. Personal expression is viewed as
an end in itself; it is living at its best and fullest. Independence of thought and action are defended largely on social
grounds: a democratic society thrives best when its citizens
are able to arrive at their own decisions rather than when
someone in authority does the thinking for them.

Arguments in terms of the needs and demands of society
do not stop at the level of philosophical discussion. They
emphasize real problems that face democratic countries
here and now, and point out that we cannot expect to progress nor even to survive unless we develop and draw upon
the creative potentialities of the entire population. This is
partly a problem of identifying creative talent, but it also
is one of exploring the nature of productive thinking and of
finding better ways of cultivating it.[1]

One could cite many articles and studies which deplore
the neglect of synthesis objectives. A fairly common theme
is that current programs overemphasize activities in which
the learner functions as a consumer and critic of ideas

---

[1] Recent writing and research on creativeness and
productive thinking (which overlap with synthetic abilities)
attest to the importance attached to these problems by many
psychologists and educators. The recent challenge by Allison
Davis and others is worth noting at this point. Allison Davis
and Robert D. Hess, "What About IQs?" Journal of the National Education Association 38 (Nov., 1949), pp. 604-605.
Kenneth Eells and others, Intelligence and Cultural Differences, Chicago: University of Chicago Press, 1951, xii 388.
After demonstrating that conventional intelligence tests un-
derrate the ability of children from lower socio-economic
levels, they conclude that we are depriving ourselves of un-
tapped resources of human ability and robbing such children
of their right to full development. Furthermore, because
most pupils get limited experience in genuine problem solving, these investigators believe that present programs retard
pupils of low occupational groups by two years, on the average, after they have been in school only four years! Certainly this indictment demands serious attention.

rather than those in which he functions as a producer. Often criticism is directed against the over-use of objective-type examinations on the grounds that these forms do not force the student to produce original ideas or to organize them. Whether or not this argument is defensible is a matter to be decided by further study; in any case, however, lack of appropriate practice must surely account for many shortcomings in the development of synthesis abilities.

The psychology of learning provides another important source of criteria for judging the worth of synthesis objectives. Especially important are those criteria relating to multiple outcomes and the permanence of learning. It is probable that tasks involving synthesis objectives provide a wider kind of experience than those involving mainly acquisition of ideas. In elementary school science, for example, pupils may work as a group defining important problems dealing with combustion, proposing hypotheses to account for combustion phenomena, planning simple experiments to test these ideas, and actually carrying out the experiments either individually or in small groups. Such activities should foster productive thinking, some independence in approach as well as co-operativeness, knowledge of combustion phenomena, knowledge of scientific method, and perhaps most important, some skill with scientific method as method. Over several years, experience in this form of learning should produce profound changes in many abilities and traits and at the same time contribute to the pupil's growth in knowledge as such. Because such experiences involve the relating of ideas, methods, values, etc., they probably foster interrelation of outcomes better than experiences which do not require genuine problem solving. And this in turn probably contributes to better retention and generalization, particularly of problem-solving processes, to other situations. Evidence for multi-objective efficiency comes from such outstanding evaluation programs as the Wrightstone studies in New York City and the Eight-Year Study of the Progressive Education Association. Evidence on interrelation and permanence of learning is scanty but in agreement with the arguments outlined here.

Especially important too are the tremendous motivational possibilities in synthesis activities. Such tasks can become

highly absorbing, more so than the usual run of school assignments. They can offer rich personal satisfactions in
creating something that is one's own. And they can challenge
the student to do further work of a similar sort.

Synthesis objectives occur at most levels of education.
Some goals, such as "skill in writing" and "ability to formulate hypotheses," are as appropriate at the elementary
school level as at the Ph.D. The same may be said of the
"ability to set a poem to music." Obviously, the tasks corresponding to these objectives will differ in their magnitude
and complexity from level to level. We would expect a pro-
gression from relatively small tasks to much larger tasks
as the student moves through the educational program. Perhaps many synthesis objectives of the kind we have in mind
should be postponed until relatively late in a student's education, especially in college and post-graduate work. But
this matter is not well understood at present.

5.10 Production of a unique communication

Under this we include those objectives in which primary
emphasis is upon communication--upon getting ideas, feelings, and experiences across to others. The important con-
trolling or limiting factors in such tasks are the following:
the kinds of effects to be achieved; the nature of the audience
in whom the effects are to be achieved; the particular medium
through which the student expresses himself; and the particular ideas and experiences that the student can draw upon
or that he wishes to communicate.

By "effects" we mean the response or change in response
desired in some audience. This would include such outcomes
as the following: the acquisition of information; the understanding of an idea, point of view, etc.; the acceptance of
an idea, point of view, etc.; motivation to carry out a purpose that the author has in mind; change in attitude or belief;
the creation of a mood or feeling; enjoyment or emotional
satisfaction.

The nature of the audience to whom the student addresses
himself or his work is often crucial in determining what he
does. This is likely to be the case whenever he must express himself to a specific audience, as against one that is

rather loosely defined or not physically assembled. In some cases, however, it is likely that the student need not take into account any special audience; he carries out the task according to certain minimum standards that will be applied by those who will evaluate his work.

Obviously, a key part in such assignments is the effectiveness with which the student uses the particular medium of expression, together with its forms and conventions, to translate and to organize his ideas. The point is that the particular medium also sets limits within which the student must accomplish the purposes set by the task.

The product of synthesis is also rendered unique because of the great latitude allowed the individual in putting his own ideas, feelings, and experiences into it. In other words, much of the content of the synthesis is not rigorously predetermined by the requirements of the task; it flows from the person and is used by him if he alone deems it worthy of incorporating in his work. Of course, as we said earlier, this is not completely free expression since the student must still meet certain minimum requirements such as those set by convention and by the other conditions outlined above.

5.10 Production of a unique communication--Illustrative educational objectives.

Skill in writing, using an excellent organization of ideas and statements.

Ability to write creatively a story, essay, or verse for personal pleasure, or for the entertainment or information of others.

Ability to tell a personal experience effectively.

Ability to make extemporaneous speeches.

Ability to write simple musical compositions, as in setting a short poem to music.

5.20 <u>Production of a plan, or proposed set of operations</u>

Objectives that fall in this sub-category in general aim at the production of a plan of operations. The production of the plan constitutes the act of synthesis. What happens after the production of the plan is another matter; the plan of operations might very well be carried out in parts by several individuals.

The product, or plan of operations, must satisfy the requirements of the task. Usually the requirements are laid down in the form of specifications or data to be taken into account by the student. These data or specifications may be given the student, in which case he may assume that they are sound, or they may have to be worked out by him before he can proceed. But in any case, the specifications do furnish a rather well-defined criterion against which the student's product may be evaluated. In this sense, his product must always meet an empirical test of its soundness.

Although the student must meet such empirical requirements, this does not mean that there is no room for the "personal touch," or that values have no place in his work. Here too, as with the previous sub-category, there is considerable opportunity for the student to put his own ideas into the product, apart from any other considerations. Even the most limiting kind of purpose, such as the testing of a specific hypothesis, still permits the student to conceive of a way of accomplishing it that is uniquely his own. In many tasks that fall in this sub-category, values also enter the picture. They are reflected in the specifications or other data with which the student works, but ultimately reside in the purposes to be served by the outcome of the plan.

5.20 <u>Production of a plan, or proposed set of operations</u>-- Illustrative educational objectives.

Ability to propose ways of testing hypotheses.

Ability to integrate the results of an investigation into an effective plan or solution to solve a problem.

Ability to plan a unit of instruction for a particular teaching situation.

Ability to design simple machine tools to perform specified operations.

Ability to design a building according to given specifications.

Ability to synthesize knowledge of chemistry, knowledge of the unit operations, and data available in the technical literature, and apply these to the design of chemical processes. (Chemical engineering.)

5.30   Derivation of a set of abstract relations

In this sub-category we include objectives that require the student to produce, or derive, a set of abstract relations. There seem to be two somewhat different kinds of tasks here: (1) those in which the student begins with concrete data or phenomena and which he must somehow either classify or explain; (2) those in which the student begins with some basic propositions or other symbolic representations and from which he must deduce other propositions or relations.

The first of these types of tasks may take the form of classifying certain phenomena. In effect, the student is to study the phenomena, or facts based upon them, and then come up with a logically consistent scheme for classifying or organizing them. The scheme should adequately account for the relations existing among the range of phenomena. At a very high level, one can offer as examples the development of the periodic table in chemistry in which the various chemical elements have been grouped according to their fundamental properties, or the development of the taxonomies for classifying plants and animals, respectively, again according to their fundamental properties. Also at a high level--but suitable for the graduate student in educational psychology-- would be the derivation of a conceptual scheme for categorizing teacher-pupil interaction during classroom discussions.

The first type of task may also take the form of explaining certain observed phenomena. In this case, there is little emphasis upon developing a classification scheme. The problem is to formulate a hypothesis that will adequately account for a wide range of seemingly interrelated phenomena. As with a classification scheme, the hypothesis or theory must fit the facts and in addition be internally consistent-- i.e., free from logical contradictions.

The second broad type of task clearly begins with abstract symbols, propositions, and the like, rather than with concrete data. The problem is to move from these symbolic representations to deductions that can reasonably be made. In other words, the student operates within some theoretical framework, and he must reason in terms of it. He is thus quite circumscribed in what he does, although the task can permit him to carry his thinking quite far. But always in the background are rigorous objective criteria which his product of synthesis must meet; subjective standards, of the sort that predominate in the first and second sub-categories, all but vanish here.

5.30 <u>Derivation of a set of abstract relations</u>--Illustrative educational objectives.

Ability to formulate appropriate hypotheses based upon an analysis of factors involved, and to modify such hypotheses in the light of new factors and considerations.

Ability to formulate a theory of learning applicable to classroom teaching.

Ability to perceive various possible ways in which experience may be organized to form a conceptual structure.

Ability to make mathematical discoveries and generalizations.

Testing for Synthesis, and illustrative test items

Special Problems

A major problem in testing for synthesis objectives is that of providing conditions favorable to creative work. This problem is not peculiar to synthesis objectives, but it does seem to be more crucial than with some of the other objectives. Perhaps the most important condition is that of freedom. This should include freedom from excessive tension and from pressures to adopt a particular viewpoint. The student should be made to feel that the product of his efforts need not conform to the views of the instructor, or the community, or some other authority, if such freedom is otherwise consistent with the nature of the task. If the effort is to be rather creative, the student should also have considerable freedom of activity--freedom to determine his own purposes, freedom to determine the materials or other elements that go into the final product, and freedom to determine the specifications which the synthesis should meet. Creativity seems to be fostered by such conditions. Too much control and too detailed instructions, on the other hand, seem to stifle productivity. Time is another important condition. Many synthesis tasks require far more time than an hour or two; the product is likely to emerge only after the student spends considerable time familiarizing himself with the task, exploring different approaches, interpreting and analyzing relevant materials, and trying out various schemes of organization. In some situations, the examiner can shorten this period of preparation by permitting the student to do many of the preliminary tasks before the time of the examination, if such an arrangement does not otherwise interfere with the validity of the examination. A good example is the essay exercise outlined on pages 177 and 178. In that case, the examiner may distribute the special reading materials well in advance of the examination so that students will have had sufficient time to analyze them and become familiar with the important ideas.

A second major problem is that of sampling. Again this problem seems to be especially crucial in the testing of synthesis objectives. For one thing, many synthesis tasks take time--days and weeks instead of hours--so that a single product usually may have to represent the student's ability. Under such conditions, of course, the examiner must consider whether or not that sample is sufficiently reliable to be accepted as truly representative of the student's ability. Obtaining a second sample, however, in itself poses many practical problems which the examiner may not be able to surmount. It is probable too that some synthesis tasks involving a high degree of creativeness require special conditions of stimulation, mood, fluency, and the like, and that such conditions tend to make performance rather variable if not downright unstable. Synthetic skills and abilities may thus be rather unstable and unpredictable.

A third major problem is that of evaluation. Exercises involving synthesis often yield rather complex products for which objective criteria of evaluation are lacking. A new poem, a new musical piece, or a new design may defy evaluation. Who is to pass judgment on the quality of the product and by what standards? In the absence of an objective standard such as an external framework, theory, or the like, the examiner may have to rely heavily upon the opinions of competent judges. Check lists and rating scales should be especially useful here, but the examiner ought to insure that they do not emphasize elements of the product to the neglect of global qualities which, after all, may be more fundamental in any synthesis.

At this point we might note the projective character of many products of synthesis. While it is true that most behavior is projective in the sense that the individual unconsciously or otherwise reveals idiosyncrasies, situations undoubtedly vary greatly in the extent to which they evoke such traits. Tasks calling for synthesis of materials, ideas, and the like would seem to provide an excellent means of encouraging projection. The writing of an essay, for example, is more than an expression of skill in writing; it is an expression of the writer's personality. Thus it may reveal not only peculiarities of language usage, but also attitudes toward various issues, feelings about the self, and so on. The product bears the stamp of the person.[2] Clinical psychologists have long been interested in such personal products as a means of studying personality, but instructors make comparatively little systematic use of them for that purpose. It is probable that educational research will make increasing use of personal products as a method of studying personality development and various subtle changes that take place during the course of learning. Such efforts will call for refinements in our methods of appraisal.

A fourth major problem worth noting is the practical problem of administration. Special materials and equipment are often necessary, even when the examination is administered to a group. A synthesis task in architectural design or musical composition would require individual equipment to a greater extent than would be needed for tasks involving analysis. Materials to be used for analysis by a class can often be printed, recorded, or otherwise reproduced so that the entire group may work with a single specimen or copy. In many cases, too, exercises calling for synthesis can only be properly administered on an individual basis, and this practice is quite costly.

Occasionally examiners have resorted to indirect methods of testing synthesis objectives. For example, some published tests attempt to measure effectiveness of expression, particularly ability to organize ideas, through multiple-choice items. Thus the test may ask the student to rearrange a group of sentences to form a coherent paragraph, or a group of paragraphs to form a coherent essay. If such indirect methods can be shown to yield valid indexes of the behaviors in question, then some of the practical problems of administration can be overcome and economies can be realized.

---

[2] Studies by Allport and others have shown that style of writing is rather consistent and can be identified with considerable accuracy. Cf. F. H. Allport, L. Walker, and E. Lathers, "Written Compositions and Characteristics of Personality," Archives of Psychology, 26, (1934), No. 173, p. 82.

Thus we recognize that short-answer questions may not be testing synthesis directly, even though they are intended to evoke the sorts of operations we would regard as acts of synthesis. It is quite possible that short-answer questions may indirectly appraise such abilities. Whether or not they can is, of course, an empirical matter. At the present time, we cannot give a generalization on this point. Only further research can do that.

Types of Errors

In general, a synthesis is faulty to the extent that it lacks "goodness of fit" to the requirements of the problem. Faulty synthesis may be due to one or more of the following factors, many of which seem to reflect faulty comprehension and analysis:

Misinterpreting the purpose or nature of the problem.

Misinterpreting the nature of important elements and their interrelations. Confusing basic and subordinate elements.

Omitting important elements.

Applying irrelevant or inaccurate elements.

Over-organizing the synthesis, so that the result is too artificial or inflexible to satisfy varying requirements, as with a plan of investigation or an architectural design.

Otherwise failing to satisfy the requirements of an external theory, framework, or of some other standard.

5.00 - SYNTHESIS -- ILLUSTRATIVE TEST ITEMS

5.10 Production of a unique communication

Directions for the Essay
(Time: 3 hours)

1. (Note: Students were given a number of short passages dealing with the problem.)

DIRECTIONS: Write a unified paper on some restricted aspects of the question of the future of private property in America. The paper may be either an argument in support of some form of ownership which you favor, or an attack upon some form which you oppose, or both. It must, however, observe the following stipulations:

It must include a discussion of the moral bases and social effects of the kind of ownership which you favor or wish to attack. For example, what ultimate right has anyone to claim anything as his own? What should he be allowed to do with what he owns? How should such rights be achieved, or protected, or limited? What will be the effects on society of the policies which you discuss?

It must relate your thesis to the arguments pro and con of the passages distributed before the examination which are relevant to your position. It must not merely report what these passages said in the order in which they were printed. In the course of developing your own position you must make use of the arguments which support it and refute the arguments which oppose it.

It must show some application of your theoretical position to one or more examples of property rights drawn from your own experience, observation, or reading. The following examples may suggest possibilities: private property in the family, or in the dormitory; rented, owned, and cooperative housing; public and private schools; independent, chain, and cooperative stores; making the University Bookstore a cooperative; municipal ownership of utilities and transportation; nationalization of banks, coal mines, railroads, and communications; national developments such as TVA; the rights of capital, management, labor, and consumers in the control of large corporations, etc.

In form, the paper must be an argument. It must not be a mere assertion of your opinions supported by a description of the practices which you favor. It must give reasons for the position which you favor and against the positions which you oppose. The reasoning must be logical, but it need not make explicit reference to logical forms.

The argument should be clear, interesting, and acceptable to the audience to which it is addressed. In a preliminary paragraph, separate from the rest of the paper, describe briefly the traits of your audience which you intend to keep in mind while writing your paper.

The paper must be effectively organized and well written. It must not follow the points given above as a writing outline. It must not ignore them, however. Students are expected to deal with the assignment.

The nature of the opinions expressed in this paper will have no effect on grades, and will never be revealed. Papers will be read only by members of the English 3 staff, and only after the names of the writers have been removed.

It will be wise to spend about half an hour thinking about the assignment and planning the paper, and to reserve half an hour at the end to read over and revise what you have written. Do not attempt more than you can treat adequately in two hours of writing. A careful limitation of the scope of the paper is one mark of a good essay. The examination booklet has been enlarged; if possible, confine your essay to one booklet. The first pages may be used for notes, an outline, or a rough draft; but draw lines through this material to indicate that it is not part of the finished essay. Please write in ink, and as legibly as you can. Since there will not be time to make a fair copy of the essay in its final form, portions may be crossed out and corrections inserted between the lines and in the margins, but please make the corrections as clearly and neatly as possible. Dictionaries may be used, and any notes which you have written on your copy of the Passages for Study.

****

The preceding exercise qualifies as a synthesis task because the student must achieve a novel organization of ideas. While he may have many ideas on the topic, and these may represent a consistent viewpoint, he probably cannot produce from memory a coherent argument which will satisfy the specific stipulations of this assignment. He must relate his argument to some specific reading passages distributed before the examination; he must apply knowledge drawn from his own experience; he must consider related problems; and he must develop a reasoned position with a specific audience in mind. In other words, he must undertake a detailed analysis before he can begin to organize his ideas into a coherent argument.

2. The following exercises can be used to test the ability to make up short stories. Each may be given as an oral or written exercise, with or without much preparation on the part of the storyteller.

"Think of some time in your own life when you were up against a difficulty, something that stood in your way and had to be overcome. Make up a story around this difficulty and tell it to the class."

"Think of a plot based upon an obstacle that could occur between the following two sentences, and then develop a short story using these sentences and your plot."

> It was an event to be honored with a party, preferably a surprise party... "It was a surprise, all right--a surprise all the way around!"

****

Here the student draws upon past experience for suitable ideas. He must produce and organize these to achieve such effects as build-up and climax.

3. The exercises below can be used to test the ability to write poetry. The student may be given a line and asked to complete a verse, or he may be given a verse and asked to write a second verse.

"I saw old autumn in the misty morn" [3]   (Add three lines to complete this verse.)

"Shining like slugs,
The cars came fast;
Across the night
Their glances glowed;
With purring hearts
Approached and passed"

(Finish this description of cars at night by adding two lines.)

"Men cannot swim
As fishes do,
They only slave
A hard way through."

(Add a second verse of four lines.)

****

Here also the student must achieve a novel organization of ideas. He must produce and organize them to form a whole consistent with the parts already given.

4. A variety of exercises ranging from the fairly simple to the fairly complex can be used in the schools to test ability to compose music:

Set a poem to music. (An appropriate one can be furnished the student.)

Write a simple melodic line.

Write a composition with a single tonal base.

Write a composition using two tonal levels.

Write a specific work in a larger form for any of the accepted mediums of expression such as a chamber group, orchestra, chorus, or piano. The composition should be of at least ten minutes' duration and have received performance. Suggested designs are as follows: a string quartet, a trio, or a sonata for violin or violoncello and piano, or a work for full orchestra, or a dramatic work or a cantata for solos, chorus, and orchestra of at least fifteen minutes' duration. (Thesis requirement for master's degree in music.)

****

All of these exercises seem to qualify as synthesis tasks. They require a novel product--something that the student cannot produce as a whole from memory. While the elements in this case are musical tones, and thus seem to be sensory in character, their arrangement into combinations of tones and themes seems to represent a genuine intellectual effort. The process of composing seems to involve the testing of tones and combinations of tones against each other, as well

---

[3] R. M. W. Travers, "The Evaluation of the Outcomes of Teaching in English," Journal of Experimental Education, Vol. XXVII, 1948, pp. 325-333.

as against the requirements of a particular type of music. In the case of the first exercise above, the composer must comprehend the elements in the poem--particular ideas, moods, etc.,--and try to embody them in his music. When such a stimulus is not furnished, of course, the composer must draw these elements from his own experience.

5.20 Production of a plan, or proposed set of operations

5. Several authorities were asked to participate in a round table discussion of juvenile delinquency. They were given the following data about City X and for three of the communities, A, B, and C within City X.

	For City X as a whole	For Community A	For Community B	For Community C
Juvenile Delinquency Rate (annual arrests per 100 persons aged 5-19)	4.24	18.1	1.3	4.1
Average Monthly Rental	$60.00	$42.00	$100.00	$72.00
Infant Death Rate (per 1000 births)	52.3	76.0	32.1	56.7
Birth Rate (per 1000 inhabitants)	15.5	16.7	10.1	15.4

In addition, they were told that in Community A the crimes against property (burglary, etc.) constituted a relatively higher proportion of the total juvenile offenses than in Communities B and C, where crimes against persons (assault, etc.) were relatively greater.

(1) How would you explain the differences in these juvenile delinquency rates in light of the above data? (You may make use of any theory or material presented in the course.)

(2) In light of your explanation of the data what proposals would you make for reducing the juvenile delinquency rate in each of the three communities?

****

Conceivably, both questions of this exercise could qualify as primarily synthesis tasks. The first might be considered as a demand for hypothesis formulation, provided the phenomena reported upon have not been previously studied. Ordinarily, however, this task would represent application of generalizations acquired in social studies courses. The response to the second question would depend closely on the kind of explanation given to the first. The first question sets the framework within which the student makes his proposals. Again, if proposals have not been developed in a course, the student must produce some which are consistent with his analysis of factors associated with delinquency. It is this process of selecting and organizing means (courses of action) in relation to the desired ends (control or reduction of delinquency) that qualifies the task as synthesis.

- - - - - -

6. Design a simple drill jig for performing the last operation in the production of the part shown in the accompanying drawing. The last operation is to "drill all holes." One thousand parts only are to be made and XLO bushings 1/2" O.D. and 1/2" long are to be used.[4] (Design not shown)

This exercise represents synthesis because the student must combine two sorts of elements to produce a novel product: (1) specifications for the device, and (2) principles of design. The student has some freedom in designing the device, provided it will perform the required job satisfactorily. - - - - - -

7. A Problem in Chemical Process Design

The following problem was used in a course in chemical engineering. The student must prepare a process design which meets the specifications outlined in the accompanying letter.

AJAX PETROLEUM CORPORATION
Office of the Chief Engineer

March 5, 1951

To Process Engineering Division:

Our management has decided to increase the output of aviation gasoline base stock from our East Chicago Refinery. The only major addition to the refinery necessary will be a butane isomerization unit. The engineering schedule requires that the process engineering and cost estimate must be completed and the information transmitted to the Mechanical Engineering Department by April 4, 1951. The process design should be in our usual report form and include a flow diagram, utilities required, equipment specifications, instrumentation, and drawings of the plot plan and elevation. The isomerization process is to be selected by you, and your choice should be supported by adequate arguments and description.

Will you please proceed according to your best judgment based upon the attached conditions.

Very truly yours,

AJAX PETROLEUM CORPORATION

---

[4] From The Measurement of Understanding, The Forty-Fifth Yearbook of the National Society for the Study of Education, Part I, Chicago: The University of Chicago Press, 1946, pp. 299-300.

This problem and an accompanying check list were developed by E. Rosenthal, Brooklyn Technical High School.

A Problem in Chemical Process Design (continued)

    Ajax Petroleum Corporation
    1000 BFSD Butane Isomerization Unit
    East Chicago, Illinois
    Job. 774

Site: 175 feet x 150 feet, level at NE corner of catalytic unit.
        Soil bearing load 3000 lbs./sq. ft. 6 feet below grade.

Feed Stock:

    Source: De-ethanized catalytic cracker gas.

    Pressure: 275 psig at battery limits.

    Composition: lbs./hour

	lbs./hour
ethane	30
propane	2850
iso-butane	4560
n-butane	845
pentane	750
propylene	80
butylenes	140
water	saturated

Yield: 1000 bbl./stream day 98% isobutane

Storage: 30 days product storage required

Utilities: water: available at 40 psig
                    72°F maximum summer temperature,
                    37°F minimum winter temperature.

Electricity: 110 v single phase and 220/440 3 phase.

Steam: 250 psig - 50°F superheat
       5 psig - saturated

                        ****

    This problem involves synthesis of a number of elements: steps in the chemical process, conditions of operation, utilities required, equipment specifications, and instrumentation. Some of these element are given the student; others he must determine through proper anal sis and through application of principles. He must consider the abo elements in relation to one another and to the requirements of the pro cess design, and he must support his solution by adequate arguments. While analysis and application enter this exercise to a great extent, the student must organize a variety of ideas in order to accomplish the design.

5.30 Derivation of a set of abstract relations

8. Facts: Dry gases X and Y react readily when mixed in a glass flask.
If, however, just before the gases are introduced, the flask is heated
strongly and cooled, no reaction takes place. If a copper container is
used, no reaction occurs.

DIRECTIONS: Consider each hypothesis below in the light of the facts
above. If the hypothesis is untenable or is not stated in a way that could
be tested experimentally, blacken answer space A. Otherwise choose
the experiment which will best test the hypothesis and blacken the appropriate answer space.

Water is a necessary participant in the reaction.

A- Hypothesis is not tenable or cannot be tested experimentally.
B- Dry the flask without heating it before introducing the gases.
C- Leave the flask open after mixing the gases.
D- Moisten the walls of the copper container before introducing
   the gases.
E- Heat the glass flask strongly, allow it to cool, and leave it
   open for several days before introducing the gases.

Copper forms a stable compound with the gas X and prevents reaction with the other gases.

A- Hypothesis is not tenable or cannot be tested experimentally.
B- Inspect the interior surface of the copper container with a
   high-power microscope.
C- Increase the concentration of gas X in the copper container
   and note whether the reaction begins.
D- Moisten the walls of the copper container before introducing
   the gases.
E- Coat the interior with paraffin.

The reaction takes place by a simple collision of X and Y molecules
in the body of the gas.

A- Hypothesis is not tenable or cannot be tested experimentally.
B- Carry out the reaction in a glass container whose interior is
   lined with copper.
C- Carry out the reaction with gases X and Y dissolved in water.
D- Cover the interior of the flask with paraffin.
E- Increase the gas concentrations of gas X in a glass flask and
   note whether the rate finally reaches a constant limiting value.

The preceding seems to involve synthesis in that the student must
relate several ideas. He must first of all draw some inferences to
account for the given phenomena--e.g., the reaction failed to take
place because heating drove off a necessary agent--water; or,because
heating affected the chemical condition of the glass in some way. For
question 1, he must ignore this second possibility by choosing an
experiment which tests solely the effect of water. This operation,

incidentally, involves the application of an abstraction--the concept of experimental control. But the application occurs as a part of this process of relating a number of ideas to account for the given materials, in this case, report of some specific physico-chemical phenomenon. In addition, the student must synthesize further by considering some other hypotheses.

9. The formulation of reasonable hypotheses.[5]   A housing concern has made some experiments on methods of heating houses. A room was constructed with walls that could be heated or refrigerated at the same time that air of any temperature was being circulated through the room. Several individuals were asked to record their sensations as the conditions were varied as follows:

Trial	Wall Temperature	Air Temperature	Sensations
1	85°	85°	Uncomfortably hot
2	85°	50°	Uncomfortably hot
3	70°	85°	Comfortable
4	70°	70°	Comfortable
5	70°	50°	Comfortable
6	50°	50°	Very cold
7	50°	70°	Uncomfortably cold
8	50°	85°	Cold

How can you explain the sensation of "coldness" by a person in a room where the air temperature is 85° and the wall temperature is 50° (all temperatures Fahrenheit)? Consider the following questions and organize your thinking under the outline given below.

a) Make all the suggestions you can which you believe will explain why a person is cold in a room where the air temperature is 85° and the wall temperature is 50°. Give your reasons as to why you believe each of these suggestions will explain the phenomenon.

b) What kinds of evidence would you want to collect which would enable you to decide among your suggested hypotheses?

c) Now go over the suggestions which you have made above and select the one which you believe to be the "best" explanation and give your reasons for your selection.

****

This exercise is similar to the preceding one. It, too, requires that the student relate a number of ideas to explain a phenomenon. Question c) involves evaluation as defined in this Handbook.

---

[5] Adapted from The Measurement of Understanding, The Forty-Fifth Yearbook of the National Society for the Study of Education, Part I, Chicago: The University of Chicago Press, 1946, p. 118.

6.00--EVALUATION

Evaluation is defined as the making of judgments about the value, for some purpose, of ideas, works, solutions, methods, material, etc. It involves the use of criteria as well as standards for appraising the extent to which particulars are accurate, effective, economical, or satisfying. The judgments may be either quantitative or qualitative, and the criteria may be either those determined by the student or those which are given to him.

Evaluation is placed at this point in the taxonomy because it is regarded as being at a relatively late stage in a complex process which involves some combination of all the other behaviors of Knowledge, Comprehension, Application, Analysis, and Synthesis. What is added are criteria including values. Evaluation represents not only an end process in dealing with cognitive behaviors, but also a major link with the affective behaviors where values, liking, and enjoying (and their absence or contraries) are the central processes involved. However, the emphasis here is still largely cognitive rather than emotive.

Although Evaluation is placed last in the cognitive domain because it is regarded as requiring to some extent all the other categories of behavior, it is not necessarily the last step in thinking or problem solving. It is quite possible that the evaluative process will in some cases be the prelude to the acquisition of new knowledge, a new attempt at comprehension or application, or a new analysis and synthesis.

Man is apparently so constituted that he cannot refrain from evaluating, judging, appraising, or valuing almost everything which comes within his purview. Much of this evaluating is highly egocentric in that the individual judges things as they relate to himself. Thus, ideas and objects which are useful to him may be evaluated highly, while objects which are less useful to him (but which may be extremely useful to others) are evaluated less highly. Although utility is an important criterion for the individual's evaluations, familiarity, lack of threat to self, status considerations, and ease of comprehension may also form criteria for judgments which are no less egocentric than utility.

For the most part, the evaluations customarily made by an individual are quick decisions not preceded by very careful consideration of the various aspects of the object, idea, or activity being judged. These might more properly be termed opinions rather than judgments. Customarily, opinions are made at less than a fully conscious level and the individual may not be fully aware of the clues or bases on which he is forming his appraisals. For purposes of classification, only those evaluations which are or can be made with distinct criteria in mind are considered. Such evaluations are highly conscious and ordinarily are based on a relatively adequate comprehension and analysis of the phenomena to be appraised. It is recognized that this may be far from the normal state of affairs. It is, however, based on a recognition that educational procedures are intended to develop the more desirable rather than the more customary types of behavior.

Although it is recognized that an individual is, on many grounds, entitled to his own opinion as well as his own judgments about the value of specific ideas, objects, or activities, one major purpose of education is to broaden the foundation on which judgments are based. Thus, it is anticipated that as a result of educational procedures, individuals will take into consideration a greater variety of facets of the phenomena to be evaluated and that they will have in mind a clearer view of the criteria and frames of reference being used in the evaluation.

One type of evaluation can be made largely on the basis of internal standards of criticism. Such internal standards are for the most part concerned with tests of the accuracy of the work as judged by consistency, logical accuracy, and the absence of internal flaws. It is recognized that even when a document, product, or work is perfectly accurate or consistent on the basis of internal standards, it does not necessarily constitute a work which can be valued highly unless it also satisfies certain external standards. A second type of evaluation may be based on the use of external standards or criteria derived from a consideration of the

<u>ends</u> to be served and the appropriateness of specific means for achieving these ends.   Such evaluations are primarily based on considerations of efficiency, economy, or utility of specific means for particular ends. This type of evaluation also involves the use of particular criteria which are regarded as appropriate for members of the class of phenomena being judged, i.e., in terms of standards of excellence or effectiveness commonly used in the field or in a comparison of particular phenomena with other phenomena in t h e same field.

6.10 Judgments in terms of internal evidence

Evaluation of a communication from such evidence as logical accuracy, consistency, and other internal criteria. Formal education in a democracy has generally been extremely cautious in dealing with problems of evaluating, especially in the social sciences and, to some extent, in the humanities and natural sciences. Undoubtedly, this is in large part dictated by the fear that the school might be doing special pleading before the individual is really mature enough to be fully informed about alternatives. It is also dictated by a belief that in a democracy each citizen is expected--especially on political problems--to consider the major alternatives and then make his own decision. As a result of this caution, evaluation objectives in the schools have largely emphasized judgments about accuracy, usually with reference to internal standards such as consistency, logical accuracy, and the absence of particular internal flaws.

After an individual has comprehended and perhaps analyzed a work, he may be called upon to evaluate it in terms of various internal criteria. Such criteria are for the most part tests of the accuracy of the work as judged by the logical relationships evident in the work itself. Has the writer (or speaker) been consistent in his use of terms, does one idea really follow from another, and do the conclusions follow logically from the material presented? There are other internal standards which may be used to determine that there are no major errors in the treatment or reporting of data and that statements are made with some precision or exactness. It is also possible to judge a work to determine whether the manner in which the writer cites sources or documents or the care with which particulars are given is likely to yield a high probability of accuracy.

<u>Evaluation</u>--Illustrative educational objectives

6.10 Judgments in terms of internal evidence

Judging by internal standards, the ability to assess general probability of accuracy in reporting f a c t s from the care given to exactness of statement, documentation, proof, etc.

The ability to apply given criteria (based on internal standards) to the judgment of the work.

The ability to indicate logical fallacies in arguments.

6.20   Judgments in terms of external criteria

Evaluation of material with reference to selected or remembered criteria. --The criteria may be ends to be satisfied; the techniques, rules, or standards by which such works are generally judged; or the comparison of the work with other works in the field. This type of evaluation involves the classification of the phenomena in order that the appropriate criteria for judgment may be employed. Thus, a work of history is to be judged by criteria relevant to historical works rather than to works of fiction. A rhetorical work is to be judged by criteria relevant to such works rather than criteria appropriate to different kinds of verbal presentations. Just so, a work of art may be judged by many different criteria, depending upon the classification of the work, e.g., representational, expressional, as communicating a particular message or idea, etc. All of this involves the assumption that each phenomenon is a member of a class and is to be judged by criteria which are appropriate to that class. This also includes the possibility of comparing a work with other members of the same class of work.

It should be pointed out that the classification of a work and the evaluation of it in terms of the criteria appropriate to the class involve some relatively arbitrary judgments. Clearly a work is at one and the same time a member of many different classes. Thus, an historical work may also be a rhetorical, philosophical, or even poetic work. The decision as to the class in which it is to be evaluated does not preclude it from being also evaluated as a member of another class.

Quite frequently the external criteria are derived from a member of the class which is considered to be a model member in some respects (not necessarily the ideal or best member). This may result in the judgments focusing on the comparison of the two members of the class rather than on the extent to which one member satisfies selected abstract criteria.

This type of evaluation may also involve the classification of a work with regard to the ends to be achieved by the work, followed by a judgment as to whether the means used are appropriate to the ends in terms of efficiency, economy, and utility. This involves the assumption that particular means serve some specific ends better than others, and that particular ends are best served by some specific means. It should be recognized that the major problem in many judgments of this kind is what ends are to be considered. The ends may be those conceived by the originator of the work or idea, or they may be those deemed appropriate by the critic. It should also be recognized that a particular work or idea may be evaluated in terms of many different means-ends relationships. This may require the answering of the following questions: Do the means employed represent a good solution to the problem posed by the ends desired? Are the means the most appropriate ones when the alternatives are considered? Do the means employed bring about ends other than those desired?

Evaluation--Illustrative educational objectives

6.20 Judgments in terms of external criteria

The comparison of major theories, generalizations, and facts about particular cultures.

Judging by external standards, the ability to compare a work with the highest known standards in its field-- especially with other works of recognized excellence.

Skills in recognizing and weighing values involved in alternative courses of action.

The ability to identify and appraise judgments and values that are involved in the choice of a course of action.

The ability to distinguish between technical terminology which adds precision to a text by permitting more appropriate definition of terms, and that which merely replaces a common name by an esoteric one.

The ability to evaluate health beliefs critically.

The ability to apply self-developed (aesthetic) standards to the choice and use of the ordinary objects of the everyday environment.

Testing for Evaluation, and illustrative test items

6.10 Judgments in terms of internal evidence

The major type of behavior for evaluation of this type of judgment is that the individual, when given a new work, is able to locate errors within it or is able to determine what in the document is treated in such a way that it may be regarded as internally consistent. Thus, when given a communication, the individual can judge it correctly as being consistent or inconsistent, accurate or inaccurate, carefully done or carelessly written, etc. In addition to making an over-all evaluation of the work with regard to accuracy, the test problem may be posed in such a manner that the individual is expected to cite the specific points within it which are accurate or inaccurate as well as the reasons why they are judged in this way.

Although the individual may finally be expected to make some over-all evaluation as to accuracy, the testing problem is one of determining whether he is clearly aware of the specific ways in which the material is accurate and internally consistent or the flaws in it which make it inaccurate or inconsistent. It is possible for the testing to be concerned with relatively small problems in which each of the major types of possible errors or flaws may be tested separately. This type of testing may be used to infer or predict the individual's ability to evaluate larger works where many of these points are included in complex combinations. However, it would seem more economical from a testing viewpoint as well as more realistic and of higher face validity to test for evaluation of accuracy on whole problems which may involve evaluation of other types of objectives as well.

The other major problem in testing for evaluation of accuracy is the question of the legitimacy of using recognition types of questions. Quite frequently the multiple-choice or other recognition forms may call the examinee's attention to possible errors which he would not otherwise note. The use of recognition forms of questions for this

class of objectives or behaviors must depend on evidence
that this technique is highly correlated with recall forms
of questions on the same points as well as on the judgments of experts and other evidence that the mental processes required are essentially those of evaluation about
accuracy rather than reactions to stimuli and cues not
clearly relevant to this type of objective.

6.20 Judgments in terms of external criteria

This type of evaluation requires that the individual
have a relatively detailed knowledge of the class of phenomena under consideration, that he know the criteria customarily employed in judging such works or ideas, and that he
have some skill in the application of these criteria. In a
work of some complexity it is also necessary that the individual be able to comprehend and analyze the work before
evaluating it.

The testing of this intellectual ability requires that
the individual be given some new work or idea to which specific criteria or ends may be applied. The problem may
vary from one in which the student is given a new work or
idea and asked to evaluate it to problems which are more
specific in that the individual is asked to evaluate it as a
member of a given class, or where he is asked to evaluate
it in comparison with another given work. The problem may
require that he make judgments of appropriate-inappropriate,
good-bad, or judgments of the degree to which particular
means-ends relationships are involved.

The amount of knowledge required for many evaluation
problems is very extensive, since the class of works, criteria for the class, ends to be served, as well as illustrations of the class must be clearly in mind before the individual can apply external criteria to the judgment of a new work
or idea.

Although a single final judgment may be an important
aspect of the problem, the simple recording of such an over-
all judgment is ordinarily insufficient evidence of the quality of competence of the examinees in evaluation. It is frequently necessary to break down the problem into a series
of rather specific judgments as well as analyses in order to
be sure that the entire process of evaluation is a competent

one or in order to find the types of errors and difficulties encountered.

The types of evaluation discussed here are not frequently used in secondary or collegiate education. As a result of the lack of emphasis on these objectives and behaviors in the curriculum, little has been done to develop appropriate testing techniques. Some illustrations are available, but these are not the clearest or best techniques possible. Most frequently the testing techniques used are of the essay or recall type which do not focus sharply on the behaviors desired. They do give the examinee an opportunity to demonstrate his competence, but they do not necessarily evoke these behaviors; as a result, they are not very efficient testing procedures. Furthermore, available testing techniques do not permit much in the way of analysis of errors made or even a very detailed analysis of the methods by which such tests can be structured. Perhaps the greatest value of the taxonomy at this point is in pointing to the need for further study and development of testing techniques for measuring competence in evaluating documents, material, and works.

6.00 - EVALUATION -- ILLUSTRATIVE TEST ITEMS

6.10 <u>Judgments in terms of internal evidence</u>

<u>Given a problem, determine a logical conclusion and judge the
logical accuracy of statements in relation to the conclusion</u>

Social Security officials sometimes face perplexing problems in studying appeals for unemployment compensation. Some major-league baseball players in Ohio and Missouri decided in January that, because they
had not played ball since the end of the season, they had a right to consider themselves unemployed. Although some of them were earning
good salaries of $8,000 to $10,000 a year in baseball, they maintained
that they were entitled to the benefits of the unemployment section of
the Social Security Act.

Team owners urged these players not to apply for unemployment compensation. According to the owners' interpretation, the players were
under contract all year around, although they worked and were paid
only during the playing season. On the other hand, the state officials
in Ohio and Missouri were inclined to agree with the players that they
were entitled to benefit payments.

> Directions: Examine the conclusions given below. Assuming that
> the paragraphs above give a fair statement of the problem, which <u>one</u>
> of th conclusions do you think is justified.

Conclusions
  A. The players were entitled to the benefits of the unemployment
     section of the Social Security Act.
  B. The players were <u>not</u> entitled to the benefits of the unemployment
     section of the Social Security Act.
  C. More information is needed to decide whether or not the players
     were entitled to the benefits of the unemployment section of the
     Social Security Act.

Mark in column	A: Statements which explain why your conclusion is logical.
	B: Statements which do not explain why your conclusion is logical.
	C: Statements about which you are unable to decide.

Statements

1. The state officials are the ones who consider appeals for unemployment compensation, and their opinion carries more weight than the
   opinions of team owners.

2. The Social Security Act may or may not provide that a man who
   works and receives pay during only part of each year is unemployed
   during the remaining part of the year.

3. The players argued indirectly (if others receive compensation, why shouldn't we?) and forgot that others needed the compensation more than they.

4. A changed definition may lead to a changed conclusion even though the argument from each definition is logical.

5. No one who earns $8,000 a year or more should get unemployment compensation.

(Source: PEA Test 5.12)

6.20 Judgments in terms of external criteria

Given possible bases for judgments about accuracy, recognize criteria which are appropriate.

For items 6 - 11, assume that in doing research for a paper about the English language you find a statement by Otto Jespersen which contradicts some point of view on language which you have always accepted. Indicate which of the statements would be significant in determining the value of Jespersen's statement. For the purpose of these items, you may assume that these statements are accurate.

Key: 1. Significant positively--i.e., might lead you to trust his statement and to revise your own opinion.
2. Significant negatively--i.e., might lead you to distrust his statement.
3. Has no significance.

6. Mr. Jespersen was Professor of English at Copenhagen University.

7. The statement in question was taken from the very first article that Mr. Jespersen published.

8. Mr. Jespersen's books are frequently referred to in other works that you consult.

9. Mr. Jespersen's name is not included in the Dictionary of American Scholars.

10. So far as you can find, Jespersen never lived in England or the United States for any considerable period.

11. In your reading of other authors on the English language, you find that several of them went to Denmark to study under Jespersen.

- - - - -

Given a poem, determine criteria of evaluation which are appropriate and apply them.

12. Since there's no help, come let us kiss and part;
Nay, I have done, you get no more of me,
And I am glad, yea glad with all my heart
That thus so cleanly I myself can free;
Shake hands forever, cancel all our vows,
And when we meet at any time again,
Be it not seen in either of our brows
That we one jot of former love retain.
Now at the last gasp of love's latest breath,
When, his pulse failing, passion speechless lies,
When faith is kneeling by his bed of death,
And innocence is closing up his eyes
Now if thou wouldst, when all have given him over,
From death to life thou mightst him yet recover.

Write an essay of from 250 to 500 words, describing and evaluating the foregoing poem. In your description you should employ such terms as will reveal your recognition of formal characteristics of the poem. Your principles of evaluation should be made clear--although they should not be elaborately described or defended.

Take time to organize your essay carefully. Save time for revisions and proof-reading so that the essay as it appears in your examination booklet represents your best intention. It is suggested that you give 20 minutes to planning, 80 to writing, and 20 to revising your essay. Please try to write legibly.

Given a means-ends relationship, judge its validity and support this judgment

Essay I

13.

"The idea of liberty as formulated in the eighteenth century, although valid enough for that time, has in one fundamental respect ceased to be applicable to the situation in which we find ourselves. In the eighteenth century the most obvious oppressions from which men suffered derived from governmental restraints on the free activity of the individual. Liberty was therefore naturally conceived in terms of the emancipation of the individual from such restraints. In the economic realm this meant the elimination of governmental restraints on the individual in choosing his occupation, in contracting for the acquisition and disposal of property, and the purchase and sale of personal services. But in our time, as a result of the growing complexities of a technological society, (a) the emancipation of the individual from governmental restraint in his economic activities has created new oppressions, so that (b) for the majority of men liberty can be achieved only by an extension of governmental regulation of competitive business enterprise."

A. Defend or attack the truth of proposition (a) above. In doing this, take into consideration specific conditions in the areas of economic and political life in America from the Civil War to the present. (Suggested time: 15 minutes)

B. Defend or attack the truth of proposition (b). In doing this, make clear (i) what meaning you are giving to "liberty" and "regulation," (ii) the precise position you are taking in regard to such problems as distribution of income, monopoly, the effectiveness of a free market to regulate our economy, and the possibilities of planning. (Suggested time: 25 minutes)

- - - - - -

Given an end, recognize the appropriateness of a particular means. This assumes specific information about the phenomena involved.

It may be worthwhile for the manufacturer of business goods to use space in consumer media solely to have the opportunity to reach those readers who as business men are interested in buying his product. Consider each of the following business goods. On the answer sheet, opposite the number which identified each product, blacken under column:

A- if such an approach would appear to provide enough worthwhile coverage to justify the expenditure;

B- if such an approach would not be likely to reach enough good prospects to justify the expenditure.

14. Chevrolet automobile
15. National rock drills (mining industry)
16. Remington typewriters
17. Buckner textile machines
18. Hammermill Bond Paper

Given an end, recognize best of several means
19.

Many people believe that it would be better if our states had more uniform divorce laws. It is recognized, however, that there are dangers in an attempt to achieve such uniformity. Which one of the following procedures would be most likely to avoid the greatest of these dangers?

A- An amendment to the U.S. Constitution is passed, which establishes the grounds for divorce to be recognized in all courts.

B- A federal law is passed which sets forth the maximum grounds which can be recognized by any state.

C- A commission appointed by the President works out standards for a divorce code and encourages all states to consider these standards in revising their laws.

D- A conference of state governors decides on a divorce code and each governor attempts to have it made the law of his state.

E- The U.S. Supreme Court establishes a uniform set of practices by ruling against all divorce laws which do not conform to its standard.

- - - - - -

Given a particular end, determine the means which will serve it best
20.

Jane is faced with the problem of selecting material for a school dress. The dress will receive lots of wear and will be laundered frequently. Which of the fabrics would be her best choice? (The test should include examples of fabrics, including some rayons. This would allow more reasons to be given below.)

Check the qualities the fabric you choose possesses which make it superior for Jane's purpose.

_____ (a) Material is colorfast to washing

_____ (b) Material is crease resistant

_____ (c) There is little or no sizing in the material.

_____ (d) Material is easily cared for

_____ (e) Material is soft and will drape easily

_____ (f) Weave is firm, close and smooth

_____ (g) Material is colorfast to sunlight

_____ (h) Material will not show soil easily

_____ (i) Design is printed with the grain

APPENDIX

Condensed Version of the
Taxonomy of Educational Objectives

<u>Cognitive Domain</u>

KNOWLEDGE

1.00 <u>KNOWLEDGE</u>

Knowledge, as defined here, involves the recall of specifics and universals, the recall of methods and processes, or the recall of a pattern, structure, or setting. For measurement purposes, the recall situation involves little more than bringing to mind the appropriate material. Although some alteration of the material may be required, this is a relatively minor part of the task. The knowledge objectives emphasize most the psychological processes of remembering. The process of relating is also involved in that a knowledge test situation requires the organization and reorganization of a problem such that it will furnish the appropriate signals and cues for the information and knowledge the individual possesses. To use an analogy, if one thinks of the mind as a file, the problem in a knowledge test situation is that of finding in the problem or task the appropriate signals, cues, and clues which will most effectively bring out whatever knowledge is filed or stored.

1.10 <u>KNOWLEDGE OF SPECIFICS</u>

The recall of specific and isolable bits of information. The emphasis is on symbols with concrete referents. This material, which is at a very low level of abstraction, may be thought of as the elements from which more complex and abstract forms of knowledge are built.

1.11 <u>KNOWLEDGE OF TERMINOLOGY</u>

Knowledge of the referents for specific symbols (verbal and non-verbal). This may include knowledge of the most generally accepted symbol referent, knowledge of the variety of symbols which may be used for a single referent, or knowledge of the referent most appropriate to a given use of a symbol.

*To define technical terms by giving their attributes, properties, or relations.

*Familiarity with a large number of words in their common range of meanings.

1.12 <u>KNOWLEDGE OF SPECIFIC FACTS</u>

Knowledge of dates, events, persons, places, etc. This may include very precise and specific information such as the specific date or exact magnitude of a phenomenon. It may also include approximate or relative information such as an

---

*Illustrative educational objectives selected from the literature.

approximate time period or the general order of magnitude of a phenomenon.

*The recall of major facts about particular cultures.

*The possession of a minimum knowledge about the organisms studied in the laboratory.

1.20 KNOWLEDGE OF WAYS AND MEANS OF DEALING WITH SPECIFICS

Knowledge of the ways of organizing, studying, judging, and criticizing. This includes the methods of inquiry, the chronological sequences, and the standards of judgment within a field as well as the patterns of organization through which the areas of the fields themselves are determined and internally organized. This knowledge is at an intermediate level of abstraction between specific knowledge on the one hand and knowledge of universals on the other. It does not so much demand the activity of the student in using the materials as it does a more passive awareness of their nature.

1.21 KNOWLEDGE OF CONVENTIONS

Knowledge of characteristic ways of treating and presenting ideas and phenomena. For purposes of communication and consistency, workers in a field employ usages, styles, practices, and forms which best suit their purposes and/or which appear to suit best the phenomena with which they deal. It should be recognized that although these forms and conventions are likely to be set up on arbitrary, accidental, or authoritative bases, they are retained because of the general agreement or concurrence of individuals concerned with the subject, phenomena, or problem.

*Familiarity with the forms and conventions of the major types of works, e.g., verse, plays, scientific papers, etc.

*To make pupils conscious of correct form and usage in speech and writing.

1.22 KNOWLEDGE OF TRENDS AND SEQUENCES

Knowledge of the processes, directions, and movements of phenomena with respect to time.

*Understanding of the continuity and development of American culture as exemplified in American life.

*Knowledge of the basic trends underlying the development of public assistance programs.

1.23 KNOWLEDGE OF CLASSIFICATIONS AND CATEGORIES

Knowledge of the classes, sets, divisions, and arrangements which are regarded as fundamental for a given subject field, purpose, argument, or problem.

*To recognize the area encompassed by various kinds of problems or materials.

*Becoming familiar with a range of types of literature.

1.24 KNOWLEDGE OF CRITERIA

Knowledge of the criteria by which facts, principles, opinions, and conduct are tested or judged.

*Familiarity with criteria for judgment appropriate to the type of work and the purpose for which it is read.

*Knowledge of criteria for the evaluation of recreational activities.

1.25 KNOWLEDGE OF METHODOLOGY

Knowledge of the methods of inquiry, techniques, and procedures employed in a particular subject field as well as those employed in investigating particular problems and phenomena. The emphasis here is on the individual's knowledge of the method rather than his ability to use the method.

*Knowledge of scientific methods for evaluating health concepts.

*The student shall know the methods of attack relevant to the kinds of problems of concern to the social sciences.

1.30 KNOWLEDGE OF THE UNIVERSALS AND ABSTRACTIONS IN A FIELD

Knowledge of the major schemes and patterns by which phenomena and ideas are organized. These are the large structures, theories, and generalizations which dominate a subject field or which are quite generally used in studying phenomena or solving problems. These are at the highest levels of abstraction and complexity.

1.31 KNOWLEDGE OF PRINCIPLES AND GENERALIZATIONS

Knowledge of particular abstractions which summarize observations of phenomena. These are the abstractions which are of value in explaining, describing, predicting, or in determining the most appropriate and relevant action or direction to be taken.

*Knowledge of the important principles by which our experience with biological phenomena is summarized.

*The recall of major generalizations about particular cultures.

1.32 KNOWLEDGE OF THEORIES AND STRUCTURES

Knowledge of the <u>body</u> of principles and generalizations together with their interrelations which present a clear, rounded, and systematic view of a complex phenomenon, problem, or field. These are the most abstract formulations, and they can be used to show the interrelation and organization of a great range of specifics.

*The recall of major theories about particular cultures.

*Knowledge of a relatively complete formulation of the theory of evolution.

INTELLECTUAL ABILITIES AND SKILLS

Abilities and skills refer to organized modes of operation and generalized techniques for dealing with materials and problems. The materials and problems may be of such a nature that little or no specialized and technical information is required. Such information as is required can be assumed to be part of the individual's general fund of knowledge. Other problems may require specialized and technical information at a rather high level such that specific knowledge and skill in dealing with the problem and the materials are required. The abilities and skills objectives emphasize the mental processes of organizing and reorganizing material to achieve a particular purpose. The materials may be given or remembered.

2.00 COMPREHENSION

This represents the lowest level of understanding. It refers to a type of understanding or apprehension such that the individual knows what is being communicated and can make use of the material or idea being communicated without necessarily relating it to other material or seeing its fullest implications.

2.10 TRANSLATION

Comprehension as evidenced by the care and accuracy with which the communication is paraphrased or rendered from one one language or form of communication to another. Translation is judged on the basis of faithfulness and accuracy, that is, on the extent to which the material in the original communication is preserved although the form of the communication has been altered.

*The ability to understand non-literal statements (metaphor, symbolism, irony, exaggeration).

*Skill in translating mathematical verbal material into symbolic statements and vice versa.

2.20 INTERPRETATION

The explanation or summarization of a communication. Whereas translation involves an objective part-for-part rendering of a communication, interpretation involves a reordering, rearrangement, or a new view of the material.

*The ability to grasp the thought of the work as a whole at any desired level of generality.

*The ability to interpret various types of social data.

2.30 EXTRAPOLATION

The extension of trends or tendencies beyond the given data to determine implications, consequences, corollaries, effects, etc., which are in accordance with the conditions described in the original communication.

*The ability to deal with the conclusions of a work in terms of the immediate inference made from the explicit statements.

*Skill in predicting continuation of trends.

3.00 APPLICATION

The use of abstractions in particular and concrete situations. The abstractions may be in the form of general ideas, rules of procedures, or generalized methods. The abstractions may also be technical principles, ideas, and theories which must be remembered and applied.

*Application to the phenomena discussed in one paper of the scientific terms or concepts used in other papers.

*The ability to predict the probable effect of a change in a factor on a biological situation previously at equilibrium.

4.00 ANALYSIS

The breakdown of a communication into its constituent elements or parts such that the relative hierarchy of ideas is made clear and/or the relations between the ideas expressed are made explicit. Such analyses are intended to clarify the communication, to indicate how the communication is organized, and the way in which it manages to convey its effects, as well as its basis and arrangement.

4.10 ANALYSIS OF ELEMENTS

Identification of the elements included in a communication.

*The ability to recognize unstated assumptions.

*Skill in distinguishing facts from hypotheses.

4.20 ANALYSES OF RELATIONSHIPS

The connections and interactions between elements and parts of a communication.

*Ability to check the consistency of hypotheses with given information and assumptions.

*Skill in comprehending the interrelationships among the ideas in a passage.

4.30 ANALYSIS OF ORGANIZATIONAL PRINCIPLES

The organization, systematic arrangement, and structure which hold the communication together. This includes the "explicit" as well as "implicit" structure. It includes the bases, necessary arrangement, and the mechanics which make the communication a unit.

*The ability to recognize form and pattern in literary or artistic works as a means of understanding their meaning.

*Ability to recognize the general techniques used in persuasive materials, such as advertising, propaganda, etc.

5.00 SYNTHESIS

The putting together of elements and parts so as to form a whole. This involves the process of working with pieces, parts, elements, etc., and arranging and combining them in such a way as to constitute a pattern or structure not clearly there before.

5.10 PRODUCTION OF A UNIQUE COMMUNICATION

The development of a communication in which the writer or speaker attempts to convey ideas, feelings, and/or experiences to others.

*Skill in writing, using an excellent organization of ideas and statements.

*Ability to tell a personal experience effectively.

5.20 PRODUCTION OF A PLAN, OR PROPOSED SET OF OPERATIONS

The development of a plan of work or the proposal of a plan of operations. The plan should satisfy requirements of the task which may be given to the student or which he may develop for himself.

*Ability to propose ways of testing hypotheses.

*Ability to plan a unit of instruction for a particular teaching situation.